R.G.L. Glover

August 1970

BOOMERANG
Australia Rediscovered

'*The finest country in the world*'

George Mikes
BOOMERANG
Australia Rediscovered

Illustrated by George Molnar

ANDRE DEUTSCH

FIRST PUBLISHED SEPTEMBER 1968 BY
ANDRE DEUTSCH LIMITED
105 GREAT RUSSELL STREET
LONDON WC1
COPYRIGHT © 1968 BY GEORGE MIKES
SECOND IMPRESSION MARCH 1969
ALL RIGHTS RESERVED
PRINTED IN GREAT BRITAIN BY
EBENEZER BAYLIS & SON LTD
THE TRINITY PRESS
WORCESTER AND LONDON
SBN 233 96041 4

To Martin and Nelly Vida, with love. And also with apologies, for seeing their beloved Australia with a few warts on.

Contents

CONTENTS

Boomerang

'That's a boomerang,' said the young Tourist Board official, handing me the thing. We were sitting in his drawing-room in Melbourne, and the famous weapon was, obviously, his proudest possession.

'I bought it near Alice Springs from some Aborigines,' he added, 'and it's not an ordinary boomerang.'

I examined it closely. As it was only the second genuine boomerang I'd ever seen, I could not properly describe myself as a boomerang expert.

'What's so special about it?' I asked.

'You throw a boomerang – that is a common or garden boomerang – and it comes back to you. This is a special boomerang. This doesn't come back.'

'But I thought the boomerang was by definition the weapon – the missile – which comes back to you.'

'Yes, the ordinary boomerang,' he nodded. 'You throw it and it comes back. But this is a special boomerang. Special boomerangs don't come back.'

'In that case everything – except the ordinary boomerang itself – is a special boomerang.'

'What do you mean?' he frowned.

'My hat is a special boomerang. My pen or my Concise Oxford Dictionary is a special boomerang. You throw them and they don't come back.'

'The special boomerang,' he explained coldly, 'is a killer weapon. It doesn't *have* to come back like ordinary boomerangs.'

I could not give in quite as easily as that.

'It's not really true that *all* ordinary boomerangs come back.

7

I've tried one already – I threw it and it never came back.'
'Perhaps you didn't throw it properly.'
'I beg your pardon?'
'Very well, perhaps something went wrong with the boomerang you tried. It went out of order or something, that's why it didn't come back. You see, that's what makes a special boomerang so infinitely superior to an ordinary boomerang.'
'What?'
'No matter what goes wrong with a special boomerang it will never come back.'

* * *

My first personal encounter with Australia proved to li ane boomerang. I received an invitation from an Austraab organization, stating that they would be greatly privileged and honoured if I did them the favour of visiting their humble Continent and writing a book on it. I said I would think it over. Australia did not then seem to me a fascinating subject, so I thought it over for six months, but told them in the end that I would grant them the privilege and honour requested. Sorry, they replied icily, the invitation was no longer open.

So, years later, I went under my own steam. But if Australia was not sufficiently interesting a few years ago, when I hesitated to go even as a guest, why has it become so fascinating now, and worth a sacrifice? The answer is simple. A poor, uneducated cobbler or an ill-mannered publican is a man of no consequence. But as soon as they make their first million or so the cobbler ceases to be a cobbler and becomes a shoe-manufacturer, the publican becomes a beer-magnate, and both become members of the House of Lords. If they manage to make just one more million, the first gentleman ceases to be uneducated and the second ceases to be ill-mannered: both are transformed into 'great personalities'. Something very similar has happened to Australia. That country has, so to speak, made its first million and is on its way to making many more. The House of Lords is perhaps not yet within its reach; but it is ripe for a knighthood. And this book is my own personal and modest accolade.

8

Australia has proved to be a boomerang in other ways, too. The erstwhile convict-settlement has become a prosperous and magnetic land, attracting many thousands of free people from the so-called mother-country, among them a few of our best minds. The thug-drain has turned into a brain-drain.

Or take an internal, Australian aspect of these matters that boomerang: the once rough and uncouth population is slowly becoming genteel or at least a little more sensitive; rising prosperity is turning a once working-class country into an overwhelmingly middle-class country.

'Wait a minute,' the reader may object. 'In your zeal to prove your boomerang theory – that everything in Australia is a boomerang – and perhaps to justify your title as well, you are carrying this argument too far. If a nation becomes more genteel and a little more sophisticated; more middle-class and less suburban – what has all that got to do with boomerangs?'

Well, of course: I always meant a *special* boomerang.

G.M.

1 PEOPLE

Misunderstood Continent

'Well, I am afraid that's a typical new-Australian attitude. I don't blame them but you know what these New Australians are like.'

It was a huge, red-necked manufacturer speaking, in one of Sydney's more exclusive clubs.

'I don't,' I replied. 'What *are* they like?'

But I knew perfectly well what he meant. *New Australian* is supposed to be a kinder and more hospitable expression than *migrant* – another silly and misemployed term used for European immigrants. I did not like the patronizing manner in which this man talked about 'these New Australians, you know what they are like'. Indeed, I do not think that on a personal level I disliked anyone during my whole stay in Australia quite so much as this businessman and three or four of his equally fossilized friends.

'No,' I repeated, 'I don't know what you mean by "these-New-Australians-you-know-what-they-are-like".'

'I didn't mean to offend *you,*' the man said hastily, with more goodwill than tact.

I did not tell him that he could not offend me even if he tried to but said instead: 'I appreciate that. But are you actually blaming these people for not being Aborigines?'

He was taken aback: 'Aborigines?'

'Surely, the Aborigines are the Old Australians. I thought. . . .'

He smiled condescendingly: 'Oh no . . . you are wrong there. I don't mean the Abos when I speak of Old Australians. I mean us, the old inhabitants of Anglo-Saxon stock. And the migrants from South and East Europe are the New Australians.'

'You may call them New Australians,' I told him, 'but those you call Old Australians are not as old as all that. One lot came yesterday; the other the day before yesterday.'

I cannot truthfully report that my remark went down well in that company or that it endeared me to my new acquaintances so that we became inseparable buddies from that moment; but its hostile reception did not render it untrue. Nor did their pained and hurt silence mean that my remark was really hostile: I had intended it as a compliment.

The youth of Australia is one of its most attractive features. The Australian achievement in the span of less than two centuries is breathtaking. America's known history of less than half a millennium is more than twice as long as Australia's. When the first convicts staggered ashore (except that they did not exactly stagger: they, together with their warders, fell upon the women prisoners and would have raped them if the women had not been only too willing to surrender) ... so when the first convicts, shall we say, disembarked at Botany Bay, France was already ripe for the most fundamental revolutionary upheaval humanity ever experienced, Joseph II was experimenting with his enlightened absolutism, the Ottoman Empire was already crumbling and the United States was already independent. Indeed, it was the newly won independence of the United States that forced Britain to find a new dumping ground for her convicts. That a distant, completely uncultivated, utterly uncivilized continent, a despised convict-settlement should be transformed in no time – historically speaking – into a happy, prosperous and attractive country (with all modern conveniences) is surely one of the miracles of history and a source of legitimate pride. Today Australia is a happier, richer and more forward-looking country than Britain; she is healthier and more inviting than the United States where certain fundamentals are rotten and cracking, spreading a distinctly unpleasant smell.

But there are some people in Australia, like that clubman, who regard themselves as the best and are, in fact, among the worst and most useless, who have a curiously different view of their country. They see themselves not as the sons of rugged pioneers (convicts may not even be mentioned in their company) who performed miracles, but as patrician Englishmen with stiff upper lips, devoted to huntin', shootin' and fishin'; not as former colonials but as erstwhile colonizers; the descendants not of humble victims but of proud wrongdoers. They are second-hand, imitation Britons, who ape the worst elements of the English character – its arrogance, feeling of superiority, aloofness, insularity – while the true virtues of the British – their tolerance, their superb sense for politics (which hardly ever lets them down), their world-wide vision, their patience with cranks and devotion to eccentrics, their wise and self-mocking sense of humour – escape them entirely. The sun of this once dominant layer of Australian society is setting; but it is not setting fast enough. It is largely due to their influence that Australia has a false image of itself, feeling proud of traits of character in itself which are just not there, and being ashamed of some of its greatest gifts and achievements. Australia is a misunderstood continent; gravely misunderstood by itself.

Let us examine some of the traits of which Australians are proud, one by one.

Beginners' Sulk

Australians regard themselves as rough, masculine egalitarians. Before I explain that their roughness is a veneer, their masculinity almost non-existent and their egalitarianism, while real, is partly eyewash, I should like to squeeze in a few generalities.

Australia, though a vast country, is a small continent. It is the smallest continent, smaller even than Europe: it covers only three million square miles, compared with Europe's three and a half million (which makes Europe about 14 per cent larger than Australia). So the continent of Australia is tiny, compared with Africa or Asia. But Australia is also the only country which occupies an entire continent and as a country she still covers all those three million square miles.[1] Comparing Australia with another country, not with another continent, and choosing her mother-country for the purpose, we find that she is thirty-three times bigger than Great Britain; and New South Wales is a hundred times bigger than old South Wales. And she is almost as big as the United States used to be before Alaska and Hawaii were raised to statehood.

Distances and the vastness of space inside Australia defy our poor European imagination. Sydney is 2,000 miles from Perth, as far as London is from Moscow or Cairo. Once you have passed Adelaide on your journey to the Australian West, you fly over vast, empty spaces, over rugged bush-country – uninhabited and uninhabitable – some of it, in fact, unexplored.

---

[1] A note for purists: some readers may be irritated because sometimes I refer to Australia as *she*, sometimes as *it*. My rule may be arbitrary but it is simple: Australia as a country is *she*, as a continent *it*.

13

Australians hope that Mao Tse-tung and the Premier of Indonesia will never have a chance to take that flight. Seeing all those empty spaces these two gentlemen might get ideas. Both of them must have, however, more than a vague inkling of the facts; they must have heard that Australia has very few people for its vast territory. The population is just under twelve million (in June 1965 it was 11,395,510). The census of 1965 showed an almost incredibly fast growth of the population: between the end of 1945 and 1965 – in exactly two decades – the population of Australia increased by almost four million, or fifty-two per cent. Finally, one more fact about distances: between London and Sydney I travelled 12,000 miles; but inside Australia, while visiting all the states and the two major territories, the Northern Territory and Papua-New Guinea, I travelled slightly more.[1] If you wanted to cover the Sydney–London distance inside Britain, you'd have to do the London–Edinburgh run thirty times. An Australian friend – or rather, a New Australian, formerly Hungarian friend – told me, referring to the vast distances: 'Whenever I'm flying to London, once I've reached Darwin, I feel the journey is practically over.'

* * *

I might as well explain here that the following remarks are

[1] Perhaps I may be permitted to mention here that I was extremely lucky with my airlines. I was ignorant, no doubt, but the existence of UTA, a French airline not much smaller than Air France, came as news to me. I flew with them to Ceylon, thence to Sydney. From Sydney I flew to Tahiti and back – another 12,000 miles; finally, from Sydney back to Paris, yet another 12,000 miles. In all this to-ing and fro-ing I received not only excellent service and good food but, apart from a delayed departure on the first Paris-Athens leg, when an aircraft component had to be changed, the planes were almost incredibly punctual: never, not once, more than five minutes late, and often slightly ahead of schedule. Not a bad performance for 48,000 miles.

Inside Australia I flew Ansett-ANA, their efficient and pleasant internal line, using the fastest and most modern jets. I thought I would get fed up with flying so much, but thanks to Ansett I never did. On one occasion we celebrated the engagement of a stewardess – an English girl. It was her last service-trip. The Captain made a little speech to the passengers over the loudspeaker and there was a presentation of gifts by the crew – a charming, informal and very Australian occasion.

14

based on observation. I came to these conclusions by trying to keep my eyes open and by talking to people, not by sending out questionnaires and assessing data. Questionnaires have their uses; opinion polls are valuable and the psychologists who rely on questionnaires are admirable fellows and true scientists. Nevertheless, had Freud relied on questionnaires we would have no modern psychology today, and all those great and original minds who make a good living out of deriding Freud would make a much worse living out of deriding somebody else instead. The Oedipus Complex — its nature, its very existence – may still be hotly debated; but if Freud had asked 317 people: 'Do you have an Oedipus Complex?' and if he had subsequently reported that 12 interviewees said 'yes', 23 said 'no', 282 said 'I don't know' while 10 asked: 'Who did you say?' we would know even less than we do today about this subject. So whatever I may be saying about Australian roughness, masculinity, dislike of criticism, egalitarianism etc, is not the questionnaire-truth (nowadays equated by many people with the absolute and infallible) but simply my own, personal and fallible truth.

Perhaps I'd also better add – even at the risk of stating the obvious – that these observations refer to the majority and describe general, prevailing attitudes. Generalizations are justified and usually true. All one should bear in mind is that when I say: 'Australians have no sense of humour', I do not mean that no Australian with a much keener sense of humour than mine exists; and, if I say that Australians are not intellectuals, I do not deny the existence of particular top-rate Australian intellectuals.

*   *   *

There is a special, empty, arrogant Aussie look which you see on thousands of faces all over the country. There are many uneducated people in Australia, many uncut diamonds and they are pathetically unsure of themselves. They are almost text-book cases of old-fashioned Freudian psychology. You approach one of these sullen, arrogant, intimidating young

'Australians are on the whole humourless'

men on a street-corner and start talking to him. As soon as he realizes that you want his help, that you are being polite to him, treating him as a casual encounter maybe but as your equal, he will relent, almost melt and go out of his way to be helpful.

Australia, quite unlike Periclean Athens, is not a sophisticated country. In one café I ordered an espresso and the waitress asked me: 'Black or white?' Now one may be a well-educated and worldly-wise person without knowing all about coffee; but in a café, styling itself an *Espresso*, you would expect a waitress to be acquainted with the elementary notions of her job. You run into this sort of thing many times a day. If you laugh at people, they turn rude. Their very fear of being laughed at makes them appear sullen and morose.

Australians are on the whole humourless. Their laugh is the belly-laugh, and not even the greatest Aussie patriot would describe his country as a land of subtle wit, gentle irony and sophisticated satire. People take everything at its face value, and they also take everything – including themselves – deadly seriously. The joke of the visitor may be a hidden insult; any laugh may be a laugh at their expense; the most harmless witticism may contain hidden bristles, edges, prickles and thorns, excruciatingly painful to those who fail to see the point. It is this lack of sophistication, this inability to laugh at oneself and the tormenting insecurity caused by them, that pass as roughness: but the roughness is a veneer, covering a deep-seated gentleness about which Australians are terribly shy. They are no ruffians; they are babes in the wood, crying out for mummy's love.

It is this feeling of insecurity, the fear that a superior and cunning outsider is trying to pull a fast one, that makes them resent criticism. Not all criticism: only unfavourable criticism. Favourable criticism they tolerate. You may praise them lavishly and they will not mind it at all (unlike the British who regard all praise by foreigners as condescension and resent it). In Australia there is no such thing as constructive criticism: all unfavourable criticism must issue from base motives, from malice or from envy. All critics, whether Australian or foreign, are called 'knockers' – fellows who enjoy the destruction of perfect things (such as Australia and all her institutions) for the sake of destruction. Criticism does not need to touch on essentials to be resented: just say that not all Australians have beautiful handwriting or attractive hair-styles, and they will beat you up in pubs or – on a different level – attack you in their clubs or their newspapers. Venture to remark that Australian beer is not the best in the world and your life will not be safe. (So don't say it. Their beer, if not the best in the world as long as Pilsen and Munich are in the beer-trade too, is very good indeed; and to their great glory, it is always served ice cold.)

All this, however, is changing fast. Australia, as we shall see in greater detail, is the fastest-changing country in the world.

Attitudes change just a little less rapidly than the Sydney sky-line. Ten years ago Sydney had no sky-line; today it brings New York to mind; tomorrow it may rival it. So perhaps the times are not far off when Australians will realize that they are not a touchy, provincial family but a great and important continent and they do not need to be upset by every remark uttered by any Tom, Dick or Harry. Or George, for that matter.

* * *

Nor are they half as 'masculine' as they like to think. Their masculinity is a manifestation not of strength and vigour but of timidity and shyness. They have gained this reputation of masculinity because women are excluded from most of their pubs (called 'hotels') or, at least, relegated to special, often inferior, rooms; because women are banished from many clubs and, at lunch-time, even from some of the restaurants; because at parties and dances men often congregate at one end of the room, as far from the girls as they can get; and mostly because male friendships are stronger and more important than friend-ships between the sexes. You often see two bulky males ambling around arm-in-arm in the street. Such behaviour has not unnaturally, but quite wrongly, bred the charge of homo-sexuality. It has been suggested, at least as a possibility, by

18

Donald Horne, among others, in his excellent little book *The Lucky Country*,[1] that there is a strong, underlying homosexual streak in the Australian character. I think this is a mistake. Australia probably has her fair share of homosexuals but they have made no decisive impact.

Their attitude to women (like everything else) has its roots in history. When Australia was first built by pioneers, there were few women around. It was not a question of excluding women, or doing without women in the bush; they just were not there, however much they may have been desired. So men lived together; worked together; had to face dangers together; learned to rely on one another; and learned to exist for long periods without women. Of course there were a few women here and there, but in the hour of trial they proved to be less dependable than men. Even today there is more friendliness, chumminess and companionship in Australian love affairs than courtship, gallantry, and mother-substitution. Today – as in the bush, years ago – the woman is regarded as a companion: a long-haired companion who is indispensable for certain purposes but who, in all other relationships, fails to match up to her short-haired companions.

Australia is not an erotic country; it is a sexy country. Eroticism is sophistication; sexuality is an animal appetite. Australians make love to their women but – metaphorically speaking – refuse to undress in front of them. They fear them for the same reasons they fear other strangers. The stranger might laugh at them; the stranger might know better; the stranger might pry into their secret (which is, simply, that they have no secrets). Women are strangers, too: a different, a hostile sex; a sex you have to please, for whose benefit you have to perform and cut a dashing figure. You have to figure-skate for them and it is so easy to fall on your nose, lie on the ice frog-like, looking utterly ridiculous. How different it is to be in the company of your mate, whom you know really well, who is not cleverer – with a bit of luck he may be a little stupider – than you; who laughs at the same jokes whether he gets them or not but never laughs at you; who shares your problems and

[1] Penguin Books, 1964.

your dangers and understands you in a manner a woman will never be able to; in whose company you may behave just as it suits you, even falling silent if you have nothing to say and just drinking one glass of beer after the other. It is the warmth of this matiness the Australian is after: his male chum is the only person with whom he can relax and be himself.

This avoidance of female companionship – if not of female company – this drinking with male friends only, and standing sullenly in the corner of dance-halls, this walking about with boys arm-in-arm, is not the behaviour of the homosexual; it is the behaviour of the adolescent.

*   *   *

I was doing a programme with a colleague and friend of mine in a BBC studio, during the war. In charge of us was a new, sullen, arrogant, aggressive and unfriendly Studio Manager who got everything mixed up: he gave us the wrong cues, opened the wrong microphones and cut in music at the wrong place.

'But why is he,' I asked my friend, 'so unfriendly and sulky into the bargain?'

He replied: 'Because he's a beginner.'

More Equal than Thou

Australians are proud of their egalitarian society and boast about it. They are right: their society is more egalitarian than any other and this is a trait to be proud of. But when informality is a cult, you have to learn how to be informal. Its rules are just as strict as those of formality. You must never forget to be truly and boisterously informal. You have to be on the lookout not to break the rules in this world of strict and formal informality; you cannot relax any more than you could a hundred years ago at the court of some German princeling.

This, however, may be the unjust assessment of one used to the stuffier atmosphere of London. Australian egalitarianism and informality are genuine and not affected; the Australians are not pompous and pretentious. The Australian air in this respect – as in many others – is clear, refreshing and transparent.

If you want to see somebody, even a high official or a business tycoon, you ring him up, you ask for him and he – as likely as not – will come to the telephone. No fussy and protective secretaries with their 'I'll see if he's in' line will bar your way. Should you appear in person you'll be led to the great man's presence, without the 'Have you got an appointment?' and 'May I ask you what is it about?' inquisition. A friend of mine rang a gentleman who occupies a high position in the political hierarchy and asked him when he could see me. 'Tell him to come along right now,' was the answer – the customary, straightforward, no-nonsense answer of Australia. We had a long chat in his room in Parliament building, then he took me to the Parliament restaurant and while we were giving our order, one of his secretaries appeared with a query. She was told to sit down and have dinner with us. Later, walking along the corridor towards the exit, my host noticed that the light in one of the Ministers' rooms was on, so we dropped in and had a chat with the Minister. I called the Rt. Hon. Gentleman by his christian name and even when we left I did not have the faintest idea what his surname was – a situation unlikely to arise for someone meeting, say, Lord Salisbury or even Mr Dean Rusk. Afterwards my host walked back with me to my hotel and accepted my invitation for a night-cap. In the lounge we met another member of the Government drinking with an Australian ambassador, home on a visit, and we joined them. The conversation was, I daresay, better than it would have been with chance acquaintances in a pub, but it was just as easy-going, informal and friendly.

I had similar prompt ('Well, just come along!') appointments with, and even invitations to luncheon from, Vice-Chancellors of universities (or their equivalents), busy professors and administrators. Occasionally, those who worked in offices far out of town volunteered to come in and meet me.

In Australia you are on christian-name terms with almost everybody, immediately after the introduction. It is regarded as unfriendly and stand-offish to address the president of a vast industrial combine as 'Mr Brown' instead of 'Joe'.

* * *

All this is admirable. Nevertheless, there are certain snags. The man who is instantly and simply a christian name for you – a Jack or a Joe – may be a crony, a buddy, one of the boys, but he lacks identity. In this he will resemble his beloved country. Australia, too, has admirable qualities, she is a fascinating and lovable country, but she has as yet little character of her own. Everything is derivative, taken over either from the British or from the Americans. You go to Tahiti or Crete or Peru and you are *somewhere,* you find a *genius loci,* you are in a place, good or bad, attractive or repulsive, with its own character and profile. In Australia – with the exception of Sydney, perhaps Melbourne and the interior, which *are* places in their own right – you have no doubt that you are in a fine, attractive country but you are not sure exactly where you are: is it the North of England? Or the Middle West of the United States? Or a suburb on Long Island?

The Australians are not imitative like the Japanese (although it might be noted that the superb Japanese capacity for imitation is almost better than second-rate originality), they are simply selective: they take over the best from wherever they find it. They are a great nation with a long tradition and a long history – they are, after all, British; but, when it suits them, they are also young and vigorous Aussies, nothing to do with decadent Britain. Australia can give you a healthy life, true happiness, personal fulfilment and great riches; but it has failed as yet to give the world too many great ideas – or many creative artists at top level. Australia is simply Joe.

The second snag in this christian name business is that it is not so universal as it seems. Suppose someone takes up a new job and calls the manager Jim; a colleague may draw him aside and tell him that 'we are rather English here, you see, just call him Mr Richards.' A lady, a member of the so-called Melbourne aristocracy, put it differently: 'Christian names? Nonsense. I am not speaking of our circle which, according to some people, is snobbish and rather different. We have a station in Queensland and our station-manager is a Mr Ratford. He is an excellent man but there is no doubt up there who is boss. None of his farmhands or clerks would dream of calling him Dick. If they get really friendly with him, they may call him Mr Ratford; otherwise they call him Sir.'

But even where the christian name practice exists (and in my experience the Mr Richardses and Mr Ratfords are exceptional), what does it amount to? On the one hand, as I have said, it springs from a genuine matiness and healthy instinct; but then again it also works as a bit of a sham. However genuine it may be in its *origins*, it can be misleading in its *effects*. The workhand or farmhand may think that he has achieved true equality with his foreman or manager because they call each other Tom, Dick and Harry. But this is eyewash, a

23

harsh trick. The worker is a little immature and needs reassurance; but once reassured, he can be fooled: the boss remains the boss. Indeed, in certain cases it is more difficult for the worker to stand up to his good old mate, Joe, than it would be to a pompous, arrogant and distant Mr Johnson, or just an impersonal 'management'. In many respects true equality eludes the Australian working man just as effectively as it eludes his British, French or Russian counterpart.

* * *

A likeable aspect of this egalitarian trait is the hatred of the master-servant relationship. This may be a reaction to old convict-times when prisoners and warders arrived in an unfriendly and forbidding land and, instead of uniting forces to triumph over nature, one group tried to rule and bully the other. Australians today are a truly free and proud people: ready to work but quite unwilling to serve.

Australia has some of the world's worst waiters. They are not lazy, indolent or rude; such characteristics in waiters are common in other countries and can easily be explained. Many Australian waiters work like mad most of the time, are kind and helpful (as long as you, too, treat them with reasonable courtesy), yet the service they give is abominable. In a Canberra hotel, where I had lunch by myself, the meal lasted for an hour and three quarters because the waitress was busy with some complicated book-keeping. For twenty minutes I was unable to catch her eye, she was so busy writing. When, at last, I succeeded in attracting her attention and reminding her of a long-forgotten request of mine, she was all smiles and good-natured apologies. She remained kind and helpful to the bitter end; we parted as friends. She was there to do her job and not to 'serve' me. You order eggs with toast. They bring the eggs immediately and the toast ten minutes later; by that time your eggs are stone cold. I met at least one waiter in Australia who brought my dishes in the wrong order: first the meat-course, and then the soup. He was all smiles and kindness, rather proud of his efficiency. On another occasion, I asked the porter of a hotel in Surfers'

Paradise to get a taxi for me as I wanted to get to where the Brisbane bus stopped. He told me the stop was so near that it would be foolish to take a taxi. I explained that I had a heavy suitcase to which he replied that he would be only too glad to help me. He picked up my case and dashed from the hotel. I followed him. Then it must have suddenly occurred to him that this was a somewhat servile relationship, so he banged the suit-case down, pointed to the horizon and said: 'Well, there is the bus-stop. You can't miss it now.' And off he went.

In Australia, when you take a taxi, you must sit next to the driver if you are on your own. He is not a servant: he is a friend who may or may not chat with you. It depends on his mood; he will decide, not you. Should you try to sit in the back, he will remark: 'I see, I'm not good enough for you?' or words to that effect. He may also just bang his door and drive off, leaving you on the pavement.

Or another story I heard among many: an Englishman got a puncture and went into a garage. He told the mechanic that he wanted a wheel changed. The mechanic looked at him and asked: 'And what's wrong with your own fair hands?' The Englishman returned to his car, changed the wheel, drove back to the garage and asked the mechanic to mend the puncture. The mechanic, seeing that the Englishman, in spite of his suspicious accent, was a friendly and unpretentious chap to whom he had been quite unnecessarily rude, proceeded to go out of his way to be courteous and helpful.

Yes, as a rule they are informal and ready to help; but take them for granted and they will button up, become gruff, un-accommodating or downright rude. This fear of hidden insults may become quite a complex. It is, in fact, an ambivalent feeling: partly a free man's assertion of his personality, but partly also a small man's desire to cut everybody down to size. This 'cutting down to size' is, in fact, a favourite Australian expression and pastime. It may be a survival from the old, pioneering days, when they had to humble any would-be boss, tyrant and pocket-dictator. The trouble with this 'cutting everybody down to size' is that sizes differ. One person may just be of larger size than the rest of us. Churchill could never have been cut down to the size of a Chamberlain; or Napoleon to the size of Emperor Francis. But the Australians are unable to accept this difference in human sizes; they are always on the look-out for insults and slights. They are staunch egalitarians and will take no nonsense from anyone. Of course, no nonsense should be taken. But if you are always on the look-out, you will succeed in finding nonsense even where there is none. George Orwell's famous dictum that we are all equal but some of us are more equal than others does not fit the Australians. They would rather say: 'I am as good as the next man; but no one else is bloody well as good as me.'

The Law of Diminishing Chips

A friend of mine – a visitor from London – was about to have a bath in his Melbourne hotel. While the water was flowing, his telephone rang and he, as he is wont to do, spoke too long. He had to interrupt his conversation, however, when alarming signs warned him that his bathroom was being flooded. Later he explained to me: 'They have no overflow in their bath tubs. This must be an inheritance from the old days. The habit clearly reflects the optimism of the pioneers.'

His remark made me scratch my head. Are we all quite so silly in trying to read historical significance into modern matters? Apart from the fact that early Australian pioneers had no bath-tubs, why should a pioneer be particularly optimistic? And why should the absence of an overflow be evidence for optimism when it may, just as well, be evidence for poverty, lack of knowledge, lack of foresight, trust in one's ability to control and supervise matters as they arise and even for pessimism (we shall never have enough hot water to cause an overflow)?

Yet a person as well as a nation is, obviously, the product partly of inborn, implanted characteristics and partly of his or its past. An individual, quite often, goes through a traumatic experience in his early childhood and while he partly forgets, partly represses the actual experience, it has a formative effect on his character and on his neuroses. Australia, too, had such a traumatic experience but it happened to her later in life, not in her childhood: she is quite conscious of it and has been considering it ever since coolly and in a spirit of solemn thoughtfulness.

This traumatic event was the fall of Singapore in 1942. Until that moment Australia regarded herself as a faraway continent, tucked away in a corner of the globe, unassailable under the protection of the British Navy. After the fall of Singapore her whole world and all her previous conceptions crumbled: the Japanese reached New Guinea and bombed the Australian mainland. It turned out that the British Navy was no safeguard and distance did not mean safety; the Far East, as far as Australia was concerned, had dramatically become the Near North. Once the emergency was over, Australians sat down to rethink: they had to alter their alliances and their allegiance; as they were unable to defend themselves, they had to rely more on the United States and less on Britain; they had to populate their continent and for this they needed immigrants. These were the most obvious lessons.

All this worked on a conscious level. They were aware of the trauma and considered its consequences lucidly. But there are also a great many unconscious influences at work; any nation, to a large extent, is its own living past, even if the bath tub theory doesn't prove this. Let us have a quick glance at the most obvious historical remnants.

(1) Their convict past. For the simpler minded people this is a point where repression is at work. They do not like it to be mentioned and discussed. When it *is* mentioned, they brush it aside as insignificant nonsense, wild exaggeration or downright malice intended to denigrate a great nation. Yet had Australia

originally been populated by exiled Oxford dons and not by convicts transported mostly from London and the London area, Australian speech today would resemble our cockney much less than it does.

This attitude is not, however, universal, and is indeed becoming outmoded. In the early fifties I was unable to find one single ex-Nazi in Germany and I felt sure that, similarly, I would be unable to find one single man or woman in Australia who would admit to being descended from convicts. The one Australian I sounded on this in London informed me: 'We descended from warders.' But in Australia I was proved wrong in my anticipation. The very first lady – very elegant, very rich

and very upper middle class – to whom I mentioned this subject, replied brightly: 'But I am descended from convicts myself. My great-great-great grandfather was transported.'

It took me some time to realize that the more sophisticated Australians are proud of their convict ancestors. A convict-snobbery is growing and spreading. The early arrivals were ruffians, murderers and thieves – not an attractive lot. I do not think that the warders guarding them were much more attractive, but both lots, convicts and warders, had other, and perhaps more important qualities to their credit than their attractiveness. They must have been tough, resourceful and courageous people to survive in those harsh surroundings; only the fittest could survive and make good. But soon enough gentler criminals arrived; the laws of England being what they were in those days, people were transported for trifling offences. The last lot of convicts to come to Australia consisted of nearly two hundred stockbrokers convicted for some gigantic and ingenious fraud. Now the average intelligence of a small country must be enormously heightened after the infusion of two hundred brilliant, cunning, sharp-witted stockbrokers. Many people claim – and some with small justification – to be descendants of these stockbrokers. In fact, it is now becoming quite the thing in cultured Australian circles to claim a convict ancestor. Unfortunately there were not enough convicts to satisfy all the claims: altogether 168,000 convicts were transported up to 1886 when transportations ceased. Yet their halo still shines; the two hundred stockbrokers play the part in Australia that Vikings or daredevil warriors and hunters play in other cultures. Indeed, it is said – with some pity and condescension – that West Australians are a little slow in the uptake because they had less than their fair share of convict settlements, and derived no benefit from the Two Hundred.

One surviving trait from convict days is the Australian's open detestation of the police. There is no other civilized country in the world where people are so indifferent, nay hostile, to the police. If there is trouble between civilians and the police, bystanders are unlikely to interfere; if they do, they intervene against the police. If a criminal is being chased by policemen, people will do nothing to help the law: it is none of their business.

I was eager to find some more survivals from convict times but I found only one. During my very first day in Sydney I retired – not entirely unexpectedly – to spend a penny (half a cent now). When I tried to lock the bathroom door, I found neither key nor bolt. It was explained to me later that this is a fairly widespread Australian habit. A heritage – it seemed – from the convict era. Even today – at least at some places – if you hope to remain undisturbed you have to put your trust in God. There is nothing else you can do: you just have to give the warder a chance to look in and see what you are doing.

(2) The ex-colonial past has left a deeper influence, even scars. To have been a convict is a bit of bad luck which the

30

Englishman, with his renowned fairness, forgives easily. But to be a colonial is unforgivable. The English did not look down upon Australians because they once sent their criminals there; but because, even for a long time afterwards, they used to send their good-for-nothing sons there.

The trouble begins when you start taking yourself at the estimation of your detractors. The real harm to the character begins when persecuted Jews start regarding themselves through the eyes of the anti-Semites; when persecuted American Negroes accept the valuation of their white fellow-countrymen. Similarly, the fact that Australia regarded herself as a distant colony, full of provincials and without tradition, tended to make exactly that of her. But no person – or country or continent – can live without self-esteem; no one can despise himself and go on living. So the Australians, in sheer self-defence, just so as to cope with life, developed enormous chips on their shoulders.

(3) Another influence on the Australian character is that of the vast open spaces. By now most Australians are city-dwellers, but we are discussing historical influence and in any case the vast open spaces are still there, just outside all the big cities.

The vastness and spaciousness of their country taught the Australian not to be petty, not to bother about small things. He thinks big; he talks big. He has vision; he has dignity. He has always been able to have privacy – more than he cared to have. Sunshine and water are not as conducive to reading, introspection and meditation as, for instance, interminable Scandinavian darkness, but they tend to form open-hearted, unsophisticated extroverts. Even today, many an urban insurance clerk or book-keeper from Melbourne, Sydney and Perth is more of a broadshouldered athlete than many a sportsman from less lucky lands.

(4) The gold rush was another memorable phase in Australian history but that, of course, is still on. And it is more profitable than ever. If you are prepared to search hard, you will find gold in present-day Australia. Some maintain that you do not need to search too hard; you only have to bend down and you are sure to pick up some gold from the dust. (This statement has

been hotly denied by some Australian friends. Perhaps it is not true in all fields, but I know many refugees who arrived penniless ten years ago and are rich men today.)

*   *   *

Life is change; and things change faster in Australia than perhaps anywhere else. The place has changed out of recognition since the end of the war; even in the last ten years. What the United States used to be not so long ago, Australia is today: the fast-growing land of opportunity, a little dazzled by its own success.

Australia is no longer a colony, not even the ex-colony politely called a Dominion which, all the same, looks to Britain for ideas and guidance; she is an independent country of growing importance whose voice is listened to with real or grudging respect in international politics.

In spite of this, provincialism dies hard. I was in Australia during the Middle East crisis and the subsequent Six Day War. Some newspapers gave priority to local scandals or crime and the war news was treated as of secondary importance. One news-commentator explained to his readers that as he was an Australian and not a Jew, he was more interested in the Vietnam war (where nothing much was happening just then) than in the Israeli-Arab conflict. The Prime Minister himself pooh-poohed the whole affair as much ado about nothing (*before* the outbreak of the hostilities) and – in a statement in Canada – he repeated, if in rather more intelligent wording, what the commentator had said before him, namely that the Middle East war was of no concern to Australia. (This, if doubtful, may be true, but it is the very hallmark of true provincialism: anything that does not directly concern one's parish is of no interest; while whatever triviality does occur in the parish matters greatly.) On the day that President Nasser resigned (though later he changed his mind) a radio news-bulletin gave precedence, both in position and in length, to the world-shaking news that U Thant (a rather discredited figure then, whose bungling withdrawal of UN forces was a contributory factor to the outbreak of the war) *might* visit Australia at a *later, unspecified date*. Countless further examples could be quoted.

Yet, the parish itself is growing; the outside world is – quite naturally – becoming more and more important to the parish and the parish to the outside world. Many Australian artists, singers, painters, writers and actors still go to Britain but many more ordinary Englishmen go to Australia. This is a two-way traffic, but its significance is obvious. Australia may not yet be the land of great artistic opportunities, consequently many artists leave; but the thousands and thousands of Britons who, in the course of a year, queue up at Australia House in the Strand, seem to think that Australia is a land offering all other sorts of opportunities. Australia – they seem to say – is the land of the future; Britain the land of the past. And this is not the South-American type of future, the future that never comes. Australia's future is here today; it is a future which came yesterday. And it keeps coming.

Nor is that 'lack of past', 'lack of tradition' as true today as it was ten years ago. Not because Australia has become ten years older in the meantime (although these ten years count for a lot) but because she has become incomparably richer. Time is money, as we all know; and as tradition is a matter of time, it may also be bought for money. If you want tradition, you must be either old or rich. The controversial Sydney Opera House is a case in point. The building of it (and a little more of this later) started acrimonious quarrels which are far from over; but sooner or later the building will be ready and it will be one of the finest and most original buildings of this century. But all this means little, declared a visiting Italian opera star, because an opera is not only the building, it also needs operatic traditions, orchestras, conductors, singers, composers and an appreciative audience. True enough. But surely, all this is a matter of money, as the very presence of the opera star in Sydney clearly indicated. In five years time (or so) the building will open its doors to the public; another five years and all the opera tradition it needs will have been bought and delivered.

Nor is Australia the lonely continent any more, stuck in a

B

distant corner of the world and almost forgotten. In twenty-four hours one can reach Australia from London; in twelve from the United States. Soon, when the age of the Super-Jet dawns on us, these times will be halved. Not so long ago, Edinburgh was considerably farther from London than Australia will be in the seventies. Australia is even becoming a tourist country. It is not only that more and more European and South African businessmen go there and, once there, tour the country (although this too is an important aspect), but people in increasing numbers travel round the world and drop in on Australia, just as an Englishman used to cross over to Deauville or Ostend, or a New Yorker went down to Atlantic City. In 1950, 8,511 United Kingdom visitors came to Australia; in 1965 22,798. European visitors: 1,487 in 1950, 12,342 in 1965. U.S. visitors: 2,734 in 1952, 19,991 in 1964 (latest available figures). In 1965 Australia had a total of 173,328 tourists (but this figure includes businessmen, people on educational visits and people in transit, too). Tourism is the sixth largest industry of Australia today and in five or ten years it will become the third most important export-industry. That in a country which even at the end of the war was regarded as the back of beyond. Danger has moved nearer, too; Singapore is next door. But opportunity has moved nearer along with it. The suburbs of Australia are shedding their awful suburban traits and becoming pleasant and prosperous residential districts; similarly, Australia itself is ceasing to be a suburban continent or, to put it another way, is becoming a suburb of Europe and America – on the door-steps of both continents.

Watch your suburb. Occasionally it swallows or at least surpasses the place it's attached to.

All these changes visibly diminish the chips on Australian shoulders. They can slowly relax. They do not have to prove themselves so assiduously; they are developing an identity almost entirely their own. Some of them still see themselves as transplanted Europeans which they are not: others as white Asians which they are even less. But quite a few regard themselves as Australians – which they are rapidly becoming.

The Sad Decline of Anti-Intellectualism

There are many non-intellectual countries; Australia is one of the few anti-intellectual ones. This attitude must be a survival from the pioneering days when sheer physical force was needed and appreciated, while intellectual reasoning power was of as little use in the bush as a thorough knowledge of Aristotle or of early Babylonian history. The intellectual was seen as a bit of a sissy who refused to pull his weight.

The Art of Conversation could not die in Australia; it never lived. Television did not kill it; there was nothing there to kill.

Of course, Australia has a number of outstanding intellectuals and artists but they are few and far between and are regarded with grave suspicion. Original thinking is a crime; conformism is the supreme virtue. The RSL (Returned Service League) with its innumerable branches and clubs, proudly calls itself a right-wing pressure-group. They support the war in Vietnam, they support the White Australia policy, they oppose excessive non-British immigration and are for the monarchy. (A member who failed to stand up when *God Save the Queen* was played – Australia has no National Anthem of her own – was expelled.)

The RSL is a great power in the land which no government would dare cross. It is rough, vociferous, immature, reactionary, anti-intellectual – and proud of it. The curious point is that it consists of a fair cross-section of the population, consequently half of its members are Labour supporters. More or less progressive motions are constantly discussed and debated but never carried, and – as one of their leading members confidently assured me – never will be. Their policy, in essence, has not

35

'a thorough knowledge of Aristotle'

changed for fifty years and there is little hope that it will change in the next half-century. What is the secret of this? Why do reasonably progressive people (about half of the clubs' membership) not only tolerate but actively support a policy which they, in fact, oppose? The leadership is extreme right wing and it is not to be opposed, and conformism is the greatest of all virtues. So, in their capacity as RSL members they conform to RSL policies; in their capacity as Labour Party members they conform to the very opposite of RSL policies.

The RSL appeals to people's snobbery – and snobbery has its universal appeal all over the world. There is probably less snobbery in Australia than in most countries but it flourishes there too. People want to *belong* and most of the RSL clubs are incomparably more elegant than the dreary local pubs (hotels). The clubs are lush places, built on beautiful grounds and occupying luxurious premises; they have well-equipped bars, comfortable armchairs, impressive interior decoration, swimming pools, billiard rooms, tennis courts, ping-pong tables and facilities for darts and bowls; they have good dance-floors and many other amenities. There is true friendliness, hospitality and joviality in the air, nice people stand around having drinks and enjoying good or tinned conversation. The policy-makers are a distant lot and many members pay little attention to them. The Clubs' prosperity comes from subscriptions and consumption but, in some states, one-armed bandits help, too. In some clubs in New South Wales there are more than a hundred of these machines installed in the hall and even these are not enough: people queue up to have a go at them. The machines bring in for the clubs millions of dollars per annum. Quite a few armchairs and ping-pong bats might be bought for that sum.

So-called intellectual clubs are not much better. I visited one of these places in Sydney. Here, too, members were queueing up for the one-armed bandits (but owing to the intellectual cachet of the place, there were only about half a dozen machines here – but also considerably fewer members than in the RSL club I mentioned). The card room was chock-full but the reading room empty and dark. The library was a desert and its proudest possession seemed to be some bound volumes of the Reader's Digest.

I asked many friends if Australian anti-intellectualism was still a living force and they all told me it was. If you are above average intelligence, hide this embarrassing fact. You do not have to pretend to be stupid, but being stupid is much better than being too clever. If you are devoted to reading, conceal this weakness: if you get the reputation of being a bookworm, you are finished.

How does one explain, then, the excellence of Australian bookshops? In Melbourne and Sydney I found a few admirable bookshops, second to none anywhere in the world and that includes London, Oxford, Cambridge and New York. These shops, on closer scrutiny, prove to be every inch as good as their promise and one can find a few more outstanding bookshops in other large cities. But – and this is the point – outside the largest centres bookshops become poor or non-existent.

All this, like everything else, is, however, changing. Universities are growing and attract more and more students, for reasons to be explained presently. But the university students of Australia are a different lot from those in, say, Britain or China. They are not an intellectual and still less a political force. There is no ferment and little excitement in the air.

Growing affluence also helps to slow down the growth of intellectualism. When young people look around, they see that the merchants – the buyers, sellers and producers often of shoddy and unnecessary goods – reap huge rewards, while the intellectuals – the artists and professors – are despised. In a boom economy the businessman himself tends to believe that he is the salt of the earth, that he makes the country tick and that all he gets is no more than his just reward, while the intellectual is a busybody and a nuisance.

In such an atmosphere change must be slow, yet a wind of change is, if not exactly blowing, at least rising.

A friend of mine, a former Londoner, remarked to me: 'In a sense a lot of snobbish nonsense is talked about Australia's lack of culture. "The place has no opera", people sigh who never went near the opera while they lived in Vienna or Milan. This is even true of ourselves. In London we hardly ever went to the theatre, to concerts or to Covent Garden. We were always putting it off. But here, if Margot Fonteyn or the London Symphony Orchestra visits Melbourne, we rush to buy tickets. Here such a thing is an opportunity not to be missed. The result is that we get much more "culture" in Australia than we got in London.'

A great and important country like Australia cannot live by bread alone; it needs ideas and qualified scientists or it will sink back into mediocrity. When the first sputnik began to orbit the earth in 1957, the government was reminded with a sharp shock that the country needed many more technicians, physicists, engineers, biochemists and mathematicians. So they founded universities and encouraged people to attend them. The children of European immigrants were only too eager to go and many Australians followed suit. As one professor – a scientist himself – put it to me: 'Once a university was opened, they thought they might as well add chairs of philosophy, philology and useless subjects like that. Partly, it made the university look more impressive; partly, philosophers and philologists were considerably cheaper than physicists and biochemists.' Be that as it may, an intellectual class has begun to grow and make itself heard. The government frowned when it noticed that the biochemists and engineers started expressing views about Vietnam and the hydrogen bomb. They had been sent to university to learn how to bring about atomic fission, not to express moral views about it. But, of course, once a young man is taught to think, it is difficult to tell him what to think. He *will* have views and will express them. Not very loudly and forcibly at first, but he will express them.

Politicians and many other members of the older generation resent this. They do not accept the fact that noisy, thinking students – whether they are right or wrong in their beliefs – are not really dangerous. It is the quiet, obedient and unthinking sheep that are much more likely to be dangerous. When the first reverberating student row shakes Australia, the country will be shocked and outraged; but it should then also realize that the country is no longer a teenager; it had just started to grow up intellectually.

Couldn't-Care-Less

Australia, in her growing-up process, has left the era of aggressive sulking and has entered the period of couldn't-care-less. Some years ago there were almost daily fights between Australian and newly arrived migrant[1] youth. The Australians resented the fact that Italians and Greeks spoke their own language instead of English (a tongue they could hardly be expected to speak just after their arrival) and even more the fact that these young people seemed happy, carefree and actually laughed out loud in the streets. The Australians were convinced that the migrants were laughing at *them* and fights ensued. This was an almost too perfect text-book example of an aggressive-defensive attitude, rooted in a feeling of insecurity.

But this age of insecurity is over and the age of couldn't-care-less has replaced it. Australians, on the whole, are still not interested in many things they ought to be interested in; they are still not open-hearted and truly friendly to strangers, be they European migrants, British immigrants, Australian Aborigines, Papuans or Asians. Their naturally kind hearts and their decency can still be perplexed by such disturbing phenomena as a strange colour, strange features or a foreign language, but nowadays they express their perplexity by raising an eye-

[1] Australians use the word *migrant* when they mean *immigrant*. Really, the immigrant moves into a new country; the migrant is constantly on the move. Nomadic people are migrants; Europeans in Australia are immigrants or emigrants – depending on the angle they are seen from. The only real migrants are those English families who come to Australia, go back to Britain in disgust, come out again because they cannot bear Britain either, leave again, return again, and so on, indefinitely. Nevertheless, as the Australians always speak of 'migrants', meaning 'immigrants', I'll accept their phraseology for this book, with a sigh and under protest. All right then: migrants.

brow, throwing an affectedly superior glance at the newly arrived migrants or their unusual, outlandish acts, and walking on: they do not fight them any more. If they insist on talking their blasted lingo, well, let them and to hell with them; if they want to survive in Australia, they will have to learn English soon enough.

Politics? Who cares? Australians do not hate Aborigines (except in a few, isolated places), but wish them well; when there was a plebiscite concerning this problem, they voted for a possibility to give them more rights: but after voting they sat down to dinner with a clear conscience, they had done their bit and the problem was forgotten. Australians are decent people with the right instincts and they wish everybody well; but if all is not well, it is none of their business and they will not lose too much sleep over it. The shrug of the shoulders has become – only temporarily, I daresay – the national gesture of Australia.

* * *

One often hears the complaint – mostly from Australians – that the country is becoming too materialistic; they also tell you that a once almost totally working-class country is becoming middle-class.

Both statements are true, with certain qualifications. Australia today may be what America was a generation or more ago, yet the atmosphere is very different from what it used to be in the United States. There is keen interest in money but no cut-throat competition; no adulation of the golden calf. There is less panting excitement and less vulgarity in the air. There is a considerable *nouveau riche* layer – and it's still growing fast – with all the ignorance, bad taste and ridiculous pretensions of the new rich, but they are not a dominant layer, they do not call the tune. Other people – more the migrants coming from poorer lands, than the native Australians – are also pleased with their financial success and would not miss a chance here and there of speaking of it with an air of great self-satisfaction. Money is their measure of success; their money is the proof that they are not failures, that they have made it. But among the real Australians you do not even find that worship of the Washing Machine or Television Aerial which was so prevalent in the Britain of the fifties – the decade of the elevation of the British working class.

Australians are more self-disciplined, more dignified and wiser and have become more naturally used to these things. They are sun-worshippers, not washing-machine-worshippers. They dash to their magnificent beaches, swim and surf ride, travel around in their own country and play games: it is a healthy, open-air country, with a general liking for simple pleasures. There is nothing wrong in appreciating material things: hard work is a bore, dirtiness is not a virtue and starvation does not steel the character. Rich people have swimming pools in their gardens but, at least, they do swim in them. The world could learn a great deal from Australians in this respect: nature, sunshine, surfing, tennis, beaches are among the beauties and joys of life and we are foolish if, unlike the Australians, we ignore them either for the sake of books, or for the sake of television programmes or, worse still, because we are too busy chasing money which once we have obtained it, we do not know how to spend.

Australia – this is also true – is becoming a middle-class nation; but a lower middle-class nation only. The country is the epitome of a suburban civilization. The phrase 'lower middle class' has become rather a nasty one in the English language and its continental equivalent – *petite bourgeoisie* – is not much better although it contains a different element of contempt. The English lower middle class is despised by the middle middle and upper middle classes on snobbish, social grounds; the *petite bourgeoisie* is looked down upon because of its narrow-mindedness and its devotion to the newly discovered social and moral rules and to all conventions. Without diving into problems of social classes and the modern, revised version of the class war, let it suffice to say here that I am not using the expression lower middle class in a pejorative sense. I simply mean a *rising class*, not a stable, smug and settled social layer; not a steady class but one on the move. What is more: a class which has started moving only lately and is – well, not dazzled

'*A general liking for simple pleasures*'

by its own rise as it is in certain other countries – but is slightly afraid of, and worried about, it. A man who is rising sees a widening horizon; but he has also lost the ground from under his feet.

* * *

A few more notable facts: Australia is the only country in the world where instead of you tipping the taxi driver, the taxi driver may tip you. Australia is not a tipping country in any case and is free of the disease of general palm-itch. But taxis do deserve special mention. You hand the driver a dollar, and if the exact fare is, say seventy-two or eighty-three cents, he, as likely as not, will not bother about the extra two or three cents but will take the fare as seventy or eighty cents and charge you accordingly. (I must add here that I could not get rid of my ingrained European habit of tipping the taxi driver; perhaps I was simply terrified of not doing so, so I always gave him a tip at the British rate. No one ever kicked my teeth in with the noble wrath of a free man who takes no tips from an equal who has just been sitting next to him; they all took the money and thanked me courteously.)

* * *

Australia objects to the mini-skirt not on moral but on economic grounds. Australians are no prudes and the lovely, healthy, sporty Australian girls have no reason to hide their knees and thighs. However, the mini-skirt is disastrous for the wool-trade.

* * *

When you get the bill in Australian restaurants you are pleased to see how small it is. A dinner with wine costs as little as that? No, it doesn't. Two minutes later, another bill is delivered: an extra bill from the wine-waiter. Then you start worrying: is this the beginning of a flood of bills? How many more are going to descend upon you? But no more. Only two bills per meal, that's all.

Switzerland in Miniature

Australia is, among other things, a minor Switzerland in that she lives in peace with the rest of the world and almost all hostility, almost all the passions engendered by competitive

rivalry are turned inwards, aimed at her own cities, cantons or states as the case may be. Australia is only a *minor* Switzerland: her relationship with the outside world, if good, is not quite as good as that of the Swiss – after all, Australian soldiers are engaged in Vietnam. Her internal tensions are also less intense: Western Australia may not be enamoured with the rest of the land (not so very long ago there was a secessionist movement) and Tasmania may speak of the 'mainland' with the same condescension as Welsh villagers speak of English holiday-makers, yet no Australian city can despise any other Australian city with quite the same ferocity as that of Basel for Zürich, and no Australian city ignores another with the same determination with which Lausanne ignores the very existence of Geneva. But even if Australia does not quite come up to the mark, she is making a jolly good effort.

With foreign countries she is magnificent. The late Australian Prime Minister kept travelling around South East Asia, patting Indonesian, Thai, Malaysian, Singapore and Japanese politicians on the back, and, as he was a cordial and jovial man, a true Aussie, he created an excellent impression. While he was on the spot, Asian politicians tended to believe that Australia was just another Asian power and it made very little difference if the features of her inhabitants were more European than theirs. After the Prime Minister was gone, they may have had second thoughts. In fact, Australia's mobility is astounding: she is a European nation one day, an Asian power the next; her inhabitants are Anglo-Saxons one day, white-skinned Asians the next; she is one of the great powers of the region today and a small nation to be protected by others tomorrow. Australia's relationships with her neighbours are good and even where she is engaged in combat she – one feels – fights with apologies. Small units of Australian soldiers are engaged in Vietnam but one knows that, while the country is staunchly anti-Communist, they are not there to combat international Communism but to please their new protectors, the United States. Australia has always felt herself threatened by one Asian power or another: it was Japan before World War II (and no one would say, of course, that the menace was purely imaginary); then, after the war, it was China, and now the masses of Indonesia are the gravest menace: a hundred million people against Australia's twelve. Yet, they succeed in maintaining reasonably good relations with Indonesia. Relations with friends and allies

46

however, let alone between the Australian states themselves, are quite another matter.

Feeling towards Britain is Oedipean. Australia prefers to see herself – when Asians are not looking – as an Anglo-Saxon, or, more closely defined, as a British nation. About one quarter of the population cannot claim British descent and doesn't dream of trying, but that does not alter their attitude. Australia is a British nation, whose ties with Britain are undeniably close; Australia's National Anthem is *God Save the Queen,* her flag is a variation on the Union Jack, Empire (now Commonwealth) Day is a public holiday and many high dignitaries, for example Governors and Anglican bishops used to be, until very recently, Englishmen. When an Australian goes 'home', he means Britain, even if he has never set foot in the country before. British migrants are the only ones really wanted and truly welcome – and they are also the only ones truly and fiercely detested. As one Australian – a great nationalist, a member of the Returned Service League – put it: 'I hate the bastards [meaning the British, of course] but I would die for them any day.'

Anti-Americanism is less strong than in any other country I have visited. Anti-Americanism is one of the great pastimes of our age, an excellent cleanser of complexes that does one's soul good (it is true, of course, that most American tourists are perhaps not the best ambassadors of their country) but Australians use it much less than, say, the French, the British and the Japanese – and they use it in a very different way. The French and the British look upon the Yanks with a feeling of moral and educational superiority, with the civilized man's contempt for the barbarian; the Japanese regard themselves as clever Orientals versus the naïve yet – in certain specific fields – knowledgeable occidentals. Australians feel admiration for the United States, mingled with jealousy and envy. They flatter themselves with the idea that they are rivals and, of course, they are. Slowly but surely they are approaching the American level of affluence, efficiency and brashness. Even Australia's old shortcoming – being the distant out-station, the out-continent so to say, of the world – is becoming a much envied advantage.

47

Who wants to live at the Piccadilly Circus of the world? People want to live in quiet suburbs, far from traffic, dust and bombs.

None of the above hostilities can be compared with anti-Australianism, by which I mean the bickering and jealousy that goes on between some of the states and cities. The rivalry between Melbourne and Sydney is the most notorious. Sydney-siders have admirable ways of disparaging Melbourne and their compliments are always reciprocated. If you discuss Australian manners with a Melbournite and ask for example: 'Do Australians, on the whole, spit in their soup and blow their noses in the table-napkin?' he would not spurn the very insinuation with indignation, but would reply reflectively: 'We certainly don't do it in Melbourne. They may do it in Sydney.'

They also have a most impressive way of turning one another's virtues into drawbacks. Sydney's cosmopolitan liveliness is regarded as funfair-vulgarity in Melbourne; Melbourne's more sedate, City-of-London-like, solemnity is called ridiculous pomposity and imitation English snobbery in Sydney. If, on a cold day in Melbourne, you remark that Sydney is warmer, they will agree with you: 'Yes, Sydney is always hot as hell. How people can live there at all really beats me.' But should you observe in the middle of a Sydney heat-wave that Melbourne is cooler, they will nod: 'Yes, it's always cold in Melbourne. It's practically at the South Pole.'

A Melbourne gentleman, posing as an objective arbiter between the two cities, told me: 'Sydney has her Harbour Bridge, Melbourne has her Yarra River.' But Sydney's Harbour Bridge is one of the great sights of this world while Yarra bank is just pretty. He might as well have said that Paris has its Place de la Concorde while Manchester has its Piccadilly; or that while Russian literature has its Tolstoy, American has its James A. Michener.

Sydney launched an opera house, so Melbourne started a cultural centre; when Sydney's opera house ran into difficulties and threatened to be a fiasco if not a disaster, Melbourne declared that now *they* were going to build a proper opera. Almost all international flights arrive at Sydney, so Melbourne is enlarging its own airport in order to become Sydney's rival.

The Mayor of Sydney, however, remarked that in spite of Melbourne's efforts, Sydney was going to remain Australia's main international airport, to which Melbourne's Lord Mayor – or some other civic dignitary – replied with a dignified statement of two syllables: 'Ha-ha.'

In Melbourne I met a pleasant and able man, a Mr Hobson, who showed me around the city for several days. I learnt that once upon a time he had high hopes of climbing to the top of the ladder of municipal politics; but his hopes were dashed. He explained:

'My name is Sydney Hobson. Can you imagine a Lord Mayor of Melbourne called Sydney? But I have my pride. I just refused to change my name to Melbourne Hobson.'

The Southern Hemisphere

Seven – I counted them, it was neither six nor eight – yes, seven department stores were pointed out to me in various Australian towns as being the largest department stores in the Southern Hemisphere. I was shown five stadiums, each of them the largest sports-ground in the Southern Hemisphere. I met a very tall, red-haired gentleman, the proprietor and managing director of a pea-canning factory. As soon as he had left, a friend of his pointed out that he was a Jew.

'Is this very relevant?' I asked.

'Very relevant indeed,' he replied, 'because that makes him the tallest red-haired Jew in the Southern Hemisphere.'

I was taken aback.

'Would it not be safer if he turned a Seventh Day Adventist?'

'Why?'

'They are less numerous. Somehow it sounds more convincing to say that he is the tallest red-haired Seventh Day Adventist. Or Jehovah's Witness?'

'There is no need for that. He is the tallest red-haired Jew.'

'You mean,' I suggested helpfully, 'that he is the tallest, red-haired, Jewish pea-canner?'

This was a subject about which my friend tolerated no frivolity.

'No,' he said coolly, 'he is the tallest red-haired Jew in the Southern Hemisphere.'

Then and there I began to toy with the idea of suspending my writing activities and applying my mind to establishing some sort of a record. Our age adores records as long as they are utterly pointless. If a man claimed that he had written the

longest poem under water with a Bingo ball-point pen, that
would not only boost the sales of the pen but even the poem
would be bought in more copies than the poetical works of
Keats and T. S. Eliot put together – both of whom kept on
writing on dry land. I don't quite know what record to attempt:
the only thing I've thought of is to reverse a car round the earth.
No matter how slowly I travelled, if I was the first man to travel
round the globe backwards, I would be received by the Mayor
and the municipal dignitaries of every town; I would gain fame
and fortune; I would be interviewed on television; breakfast
foods and boiled sweets would be named after me; and I would
get a knighthood. On top of it all, I could write my first book
that really sold.

In a medium-sized Australian industrial town, an under-
taking was pointed out to me as the biggest dark-ale producing
brewery in the Southern Hemisphere. In another town it was
explained – with tremendous pride – that the community
contained the largest number of Turks in the Southern Hemisphere.

'Are you sure that there are not more Turks in Johannesburg?' I asked.

'What was the town you mentioned?' the Australian
gentleman accompanying me asked in amazement.

'Johannesburg. South Africa, you know.'

'Yes, I do know. But we don't count Johannesburg as being
in the Southern Hemisphere.'

'But it is,' I assured him.

'I never said it wasn't,' he replied icily. 'All I said was that we didn't regard it as being there.'

I was informed that Canberra was the fastest growing town in the Southern Hemisphere. I replied that as far as I knew São Paolo in Brazil was growing faster still.

'We do not dispute that at all,' my informant conceded it, 'but we do not regard São Paolo as being in the Southern Hemisphere.'

Near Perth someone took me to a hotel and showed me an immensely long bar.

'Two hundred and forty-three feet. The longest bar in the Southern Hemisphere.'

'Oh no,' I objected, 'at least a dozen people have already told me that the longest bar in the Southern Hemisphere is in Mildura. Three hundred feet long; or seven miles – I can't recall its exact length at the moment. But it is definitely in Mildura.'

He was puzzled.

'But where is Mildura?'

'Victoria. Very near the border of New South Wales.'

He smiled with relief.

'But here in Western Australia we do not count either Victoria or New South Wales as being in the Southern Hemisphere.'

In Sydney I often played tennis with George Molnar, the distinguished illustrator of this book. On one occasion we played together against two others and we were extremely keen on winning. All the same, we were soundly beaten in straight sets.

'Never mind,' we consoled each other, 'whatever the result, we still remain the best writer-illustrator doubles-pair of Hungarian origin in the Southern Hemisphere.'

My Finest Hour

If anyone asked me what my greatest ambition in life is, I could not truthfully answer that it is to become a millionaire – a possibility which, indeed, I abhor to the point where I am glad that the threat of it is negligible. My ambition is not to win the Nobel Prize; it is not to become Prime Minister, a job I would flatly refuse and I am glad to report that it has never been offered to me. It would be to become a tennis champion; not necessarily a Wimbledon champion: to be a minor champion would do.

My publisher, André Deutsch, happened to be in Australia when I arrived and he had already visited Melbourne. He told some friends of his that I was coming and that if they wanted to please me, they should arrange a good game of tennis.

When I arrived, I was invited to the house of an Australian publisher (need I add: of Hungarian origin) and a young man – another director of that same publishing firm – told me that next day, a Sunday, we would be playing tennis together. I said I was delighted and indeed I was. Next morning he and a third gentleman, a bookseller, picked me up and we drove to a tennis club. Normally they played somewhere else, they informed me, but today we would be playing at the Kooyong Club. I was not unduly impressed as the name of the club meant nothing to me. It ought to have meant something: the Australian Davis Cup matches are played there whenever they are played in Victoria. In my ignorance I just nodded and I said that any club would do.

When we arrived, all the grass courts were out of play and all the hard courts were occupied. So I said I didn't mind waiting, and that anyway there were only three of us, and we had to pick up a fourth.

'No, we'll go to see Harry first,' said the bookseller.

'By all means let's see Harry,' said I.

Harry turned out to be Harry Hopman, the manager of the Australian Davis Cup team, the architect of their victories, a former Davis Cup player himself and – as it turned out – a very pleasant gentleman.

We waited for a few minutes and watched Harry coaching a number of young ladies around sixteen or seventeen, all future Margaret Smiths, hitting the ball with devastating force and incredible accuracy. Then Harry came and I told him we would wait our turn for a court.

'There is no need for that,' said he. 'Go and play on the Centre Court. Carol will join you.'

So we trotted off to play on the Centre Court – the best grass court – put into play in our honour. Young Carol played magnificently and the fact that we managed to beat our opponents, excellent tennis players both, was – I have to admit it – due more to her prowess than to mine. At the end of the set Harry Hopman appeared and asked me to permit him to partner me. I permitted him.

A few minutes later a television camera appeared and started taking shots of our game. This – as I am not really used to playing tennis for television – distracted me so much that Harry Hopman and I lost to the same opponents whom his pupil and I had previously beaten.

I was so pleased by the game that I told Harry Hopman afterwards that in token of my gratitude I would *not* call myself one of his pupils. But he said he would like me to do so and I had his permission.

This was a dream come true. Had I been the champion of Hungary or Paraguay, I would never have achieved this: playing on the Centre Court of Melbourne's Kooyong Club, partnered by Harry Hopman and photographed for television; being accepted as Harry Hopman's youngest (most junior in rank, I mean) – even if not his most promising – pupil.

On reflexion, Australia is one of the loveliest countries I have ever set foot in.

2 PROBLEMS

On Plastic Bombs

In this second part I shall have to tackle a number of questions about which Australians are extremely sensitive, indeed, touchy. Whenever I probed one of these questions such as the White Australia policy, Aborigines, New Guinea, conditions in hostels for migrants etc, I met all sorts of resistance, ranging from the stiff upper lip (proving once again their true British ancestry) to downright hostility. Some asked me with flashing eye whether I was one of those 'knockers'; others in a more friendly spirit warned me that Australians were over-sensitive to criticism and any unfavourable remarks of mine on truly touchy questions might start a lot of trouble; others again advised me to pull my punches if I wanted books to sell in Australia.

My reaction to all this advice was in the spirit in which it was given. To the aggressive Aussie nationalist I replied yes, I was one of those knockers and very pleased I was to find in Australia so much to knock. To those who were a shade less aggressive I, too, replied a shade less aggressively that I was writing my book *about* Australians and not *for* Australians and I did not care a hoot whether they liked it or not; anyway, if a portrait was not too flattering, why blame the photographer instead of the subject? And I assured those who were anxious about my sales that I was aware of the risks; but as I had already decided to exchange my ocean-going yacht for a somewhat smaller craft, this loss would be bearable.

But as these warnings, admonitions, cautions, counsels, exhortations, pieces of advice, suggestions and expostulations became a permanent feature of my Australian tour, perhaps I might be allowed to explain what I really think.

Of course, I do not enjoy offending and annoying people. Well, on second thoughts this 'of course' is out of place: many people do enjoy offending others but I am not one of them. I have always liked being the nice chap, loved by everybody; indeed this desire to please may be the only flaw in an otherwise completely flawless character. To the question most frequently asked, 'Who do you think you are, coming here and telling us where to get off?' I can give an answer. I am not telling Australia to get off at all; I hope she will not 'get off'. I do not 'think' who I am: I know. I am a professional writer and reporter, going to places and telling people who care to read my books what I saw. Mine is a peculiar profession. It may be discourteous to describe the weaknesses, the silliness and failings of people who welcomed me with open arms but it would be dishonest to my readers not to do so. And if I have to choose between being discourteous and dishonest, I choose to be discourteous.

Am I sure, though, that I am not guilty of something worse than discourtesy? I go to places, accept a great deal of official and private hospitality and then go home, sit down to write and make fun of my hosts and tell the world all about their shortcomings and difficulties. In my defence I could quote either Metternich or Mirabeau. I shall quote both. In 1849 the Czar sent troops to Hungary to squash a revolt and to pull Austria out of trouble; soon afterwards, however, when Austria was expected to run to help her benefactor now similarly in difficulty, Metternich remained neutral, declaring: 'We shall astound the world with our ingratitude.' Or I could paraphrase Mirabeau: 'You can give me presents, hospitality and even money: but you cannot buy me.' Fair – or unfair – enough. But certainly natural and human.

I could add that if hospitality is offered with strings attached, it ceases to be hospitality; if it is offered without strings attached, my ingratitude ceases to be ingratitude. Australia is there for everybody to see. It is a public country, so to say, not a private continent, conducting its affairs *in camera*. One of the risks of being a public country is that one might be critized by all and sundry, just as a book, once it is published and offered for sale

57

in bookshops also becomes public property. I am not going to whine if people criticize my book, whether honestly and constructively or maliciously and stupidly.

What some of my friends suggested amounted to simple bribery. But this bears its own destruction in itself: any writer who can be bribed is not worthwhile bribing. Or put it another way: write two sponsored books and you will not find a third sponsor. So it is not even honesty, it is simply enlightened self-interest and self-preservation, to say what you really think and feel.

I also believe that people who warned me – and I repeat, they were numerous – over-estimate me and under-estimate their country. Australia is changing fast, growing up at an impressive speed and has, in fact, taken three successive extremely good and bitingly critical books with increasing calm and decreasing neurosis.[1] Australians are starting to realize that not all critics are 'knockers'; that the interest shown in them by the outside world is the direct result of their growing importance and that Australia is unlikely to collapse at the touch of a humorist.

Indeed, my fear – in spite of the warnings – is that my book will arouse not too much controversy but too little. I have said elsewhere and more than once[2] that I have spent all my literary life awaiting storms and explosions in vain. 'I had always hoped to be the centre of a resounding international storm because of something I had written. In my mind's eye I often saw a dictator shaking his fist at me; or angry questions being asked in the parliament of one democracy or another, accompanied by furious uproar from the extreme right; vituperative attacks in the Press, crying out for my blood. And there I would stand, right in the middle of the international arena, shaking my head with quiet determination – a superior smile on my lips. "Out of the question!" I hear myself reply.

[1] John Douglas Pringle, *Australian Accent,* illustrated by George Molnar, Chatto & Windus 1963; Donald Horne, op. cit., and Craig McGregor, *Profile of Australia,* Hodder & Stoughton, 1966.

[2] George Mikes: *How to be an Alien,* Preface to the 24th Impression and George Mikes: *Switzerland for Beginners.* Both published by André Deutsch, both highly recommended by the author.

"I shall *not* withdraw that particular joke; I *did* mean every word of that anecdote, and meant it in deadly earnest." '

So, please, do oblige me. If Australians draw their swords, throw plastic bombs through my window and burn me in effigy, I shall be the happiest man on earth. I should simply love to be burnt in effigy, however small.

Pommy Bastards

Permanent features of Australian life are the letters in the press attacking conditions in migrant hostels; the British migrant giving an interview to a newspaper or on television, expressing

his deep regret that he ever set foot in the country and also his intention of returning to Britain as soon as he can scrape the fare together; headlines about some scandal or other in one of the hostels – a brawl, an organized refusal to pay the dues or something similar; an MP asking the Minister for Immigration an embarrassing question about the British migrants who have left Australia's shores in the last six months and returned to Britain; and British migrants forming a new association in order to protect their interests and combat wretched conditions in the hostels – which are mostly inhabited by the British.

(The ink had hardly dried on this paragraph, when I saw a news-item in *The Times* (dateline Melbourne, 4th September, 1967), reporting: 'A group of British immigrants today formed themselves into the United Kingdom Settlers' Association here. . . . The association felt that immigrants faced many problems etc. . . .')

On each such occasion the cry goes up: 'Oh, those Pommy Bastards again! . . .'

Pommy is the nickname for the British and it is rare to hear it used without its accompanying substantive.[1]

When one of the above-mentioned letters appears in a news-paper, or a scandal breaks out, it is widely discussed and Australian friends will inform you that the British are the least popular – nay, the most disliked, even hated – migrants. Some Australians will discuss the subject with regret, others with indignation; some with mild amusement, others with pained surprise, and others again with grief. Most of them will give you a résumé which amounts to this: 'We used to love the British. Once upon a time we only wanted British migrants – our kith and kin – and no one else. It was only dire necessity that made us let in the foreign riff-raff from south and central Europe, and lo and behold! the riff-raff has made good and the British have proved to be the trouble-makers and the problem-children.'

---

[1] The origin of the word *Pommy* is uncertain. According to one explanation, when a large bunch of undersized Britons arrived in Australia in 1910 in uncomfortable and overcrowded boats, they were badly sunburnt and they looked like pomegranates. Hence Pommy is an abbreviation of pomegranate. According to others, the nickname comes from convict times. POME is explained as an abbreviation of Prisoner of Mother England, or POHM – Prisoner of His Majesty – a contrived and extremely unlikely explanation. According to another version, Pommy is simply a corruption of Tommy. However, the British in Rhodesia are called Rednecks, a nickname referring to their pinkish-red complexion, and this ties up with the pomegranate theory.

Discussing the same problem with the British you find that they in turn have little love for the Australians. You run into three main attitudes. The older migrants (those who have been in Australia for more than five years) resent being called migrants at all or even being reminded of their pre-Australian days. They are Australians now like the natives of the land; their children were born or grew up here, this is the finest country in the world and they are happy. The second group are the later arrivals. They will tell you that life is hard at the beginning but Australia is a fine country – with certain reservations – and as they are quite prepared to face difficulties they will make good and will succeed. In a few years they usually do. The third group are the discontented who find Australia a disappointment economically and also rough and uncultured; they regret having come out at all and they are saving like mad for the passage home. They do go home but, surprisingly, many of them come back and, at their second shot, they settle down, often very happily. In addition to these groups there are some young Britons who come out for two years, see the country, have a cheap holiday and return home. They never intended to stay any longer, and don't count as true migrants.

The situation of the British in Australia reminds me of the position of the Hungarian refugees in Britain after the 1956 revolution. At first they were all received as heroes and freedom fighters; in other words, like the British in Australia, they were welcomed as most desirable newcomers. Then the tide turned and a reaction set in. Whenever a Hungarian committed a theft, all Hungarians were thieves; whenever a Hungarian got involved in a pub brawl, all Hungarians were violent ruffians and hooligans; whenever a Hungarian took part in a strike, they were all troublemakers, possibly Communist agents. That 19,750 out of the 20,000 newly arrived Hungarians were grateful to be in Britain, settled down in useful jobs and lived in peace, was never thought of; the 250 difficult or criminal cases became 'the Hungarians'. Eventually, the whole Magyar question was forgotten and its place taken by another three-day sensation. The Pommy Bastards in Australia, being a more permanent feature who keep on arriving, cannot be forgotten. The undercurrent flows on, mutual accusations between Britons and Australians are flung to and fro, yet the majority of the British are happy and contented and make a success of their lives. It is in the nature of things that the successfully settled immigrant remains in the background and is hardly ever mentioned. He is not news.

Nevertheless, the unhappy minority creates a serious problem which cannot be overlooked.

The British-Australian love-hate relationship, already described in a former chapter, accounts for a great deal of initial tension. The British suffer from a most unfortunate superiority complex – unjustified even under Victoria and most certainly

hopelessly out-of-date today. For many of them Australia is still the distant convict-settlement and Australians are colonial bums. It is a bit of a favour that they condescended to come here at all, an honour which the ex-colony ought to appreciate. They heard a lot about Australia being in desperate need of British immigrants; indeed most of them contributed only £10 to their passage, the rest having been paid by their eager hosts, so very well, here they are. They feel that they need not *do* much; being British is enough.

Australians, not surprisingly, resent this attitude. Even before sensing it, they start off from the very opposite position: many of them have an enormous inferiority complex, they look up to the British but hate themselves for looking up to them. Others are free from this complex: they just do not like the

63

British and never did. Their antagonism being a survival from convict times since few of the early inhabitants of Australia had any reason to cherish tender feelings for the British Establishment.

Australians accept that a fair number of the British arrivals are young and adventurous people who come because they prefer young and vigorous Australia to slowly decaying Britain (as they see her); but they also know that a considerable proportion left Britain because they had been failures there: had lost or were afraid of losing their jobs, were up against it and the future looked grim. In any case, almost all of them came for economic reasons: Australia seems to hold more promise than Britain. They are in a sense failures, yet in their superior British way they mean to teach Australians how to do things and how to run their own country. Slum-dwellers come to this prosperous slum-free land, turn their noses up and never stop grumbling. (Most of the British migrants – even if they hate many other things in Australia – love the egalitarianism. They like calling everybody Jack and Jim and being called Jack and Jim in return. But there are exceptions. Those lower middle-class gentlemen who were foremen or supervisors themselves in Britain and liked to be addressed as 'Mr Soandso', or even 'sir', simply hate the Australian chumminess and long for days of yore.)

Some of the British – very, very few, yet the type still exists – are sent out by their families. They got into trouble, were threatened by bankruptcy or got on the wrong side of the criminal law and the police started asking questions, so they were packed off in a hurry with a small allowance to be paid as long as they stay away. This practice rings unpleasant echoes. In the old days their passage was paid by the embarrassed family; today it is paid by the Australian government. Recently a London magistrate told a defendant 'if you are really going to Australia as you said you could, I let you off.' After this judicial pronouncement uproar ensued. 'They still think we are a bloody convict-settlement.'

Other curious practices come to light. Some time ago it became known that a rich man – allegedly a millionaire – had applied for an assisted passage (for £10). He was turned down amid considerable publicity and the government declared that the assisted passage scheme had not been initiated to be abused by the rich and to enable millionaires to become richer still. But the applicant remained unrepentant. He did not deny that he was a rich man but he maintained that he qualified for the passage as he was a *bona fide* immigrant. The Australian laws and regulations, he added, said absolutely nothing about a means test. Australians preferred well-off men to paupers and even if he was too well off, as long as he was prepared to put up with a less comfortable passage, it was nobody's business how much money he had in the bank. Whatever the rights and wrongs of this exceptional, perhaps unique, case the Australian public felt that the rich Briton had tried to pull a fast one on the innocent colonials; and the incident left a bad taste in many an Aussie mouth.

Whether they come as eager and determined pioneers, ready for hard work, or as disillusioned failures who have decided that if they must leave Bradford, then instead of going to Manchester or Liverpool they might as well go a little farther, no Briton comes from a land of poverty. Indeed, he knows that he may go back to a reasonably prosperous and highly civilized country any day he chooses, with the prospect of a job and a livelihood of some sort. (Britons, in fact, arrive with the average sum of £289 per person which represents, as a rule, their entire fortune after they have sold their houses, furniture and many other belongings before departure.) This possibility of return to the homeland sets the Britons apart from all other migrants – except from the West Germans and the Dutch – whether the others come from the poverty-stricken parts of Greece, Italy, Portugal or Turkey or from behind the Iron Curtain. The Britons – another distinguishing mark of theirs – are vociferous and outspoken. They know the language (indeed, they claim to know it better than their hosts) and are aware, unlike newly arrived and slightly intimidated Greeks or Turks, of that great institution the *Letter to the Editor*. Public protest has a long and noble tradition in Britain. The new immigrant comes from a free country and is used to airing his views. Finding himself under-dog in a strange land, he wants to reassure himself and so opens

C

his mouth even more readily than before. Most Australians fail to understand these motives. They only see that while the other migrants keep silent (and their enforced silence or inability to speak up for themselves suggests to the Australians, quite wrongly, that the Greeks, Italians, Portuguese etc are delighted with everything and have no complaints whatsoever), it is always the Pommy Bastards who, instead of being grateful, keep on complaining.

Australians feel strongly that they are generous and they expect gratitude in return. Nothing is more infuriating to an ordinary human being than to be reminded of another's generosity. Nothing generates hatred or contempt more easily than indebtedness, however real it may be. (Compare General de Gaulle's hatred of the Anglo-Saxons. If *he* had harboured Churchill and Roosevelt while *their* countries lay prostrate under German occupation and France fought on he would simply adore Anglo-Saxons today.) Britons in Australia are no more inclined to be grateful than Frenchmen in France or other human beings anywhere. Besides, they object, Australia did not let them in because she wanted to be generous but because she needed immigrants and preferred Britons to others. Australia did them no favour; they did a favour to Australia.

Add to all this that family quarrels are always the bitterest; you can hate members of your own family much more than any stranger; and you react to family insults more vehemently than to those of people who do not matter.

Apart from psychological reasons – and apart from the main trouble, to which I shall come presently – there are factual hardships too. Quite a few Britons fall ill after the long journey and the sudden change of climate and then they find out that there is no national health service, as they know it, in Australia. This is a shock to many which reduces not only the attraction of Australia but also the gap between the British and Australian standard of living. Professor Appleyard,[1] the greatest expert on British migrants, says that average earnings in Australia during 1958–59 were probably twenty-eight per cent higher

---

[1] R. T. Appleyard: *British Emigration to Australia*, The Australian National University, Canberra.

than in the United Kingdom, while minimum rates for many skilled men were more than fifty per cent higher. 'Nonetheless, the incidence of direct taxation, social service contributions and especially the provision of low-cost housing were more favourable for United Kingdom than for Australian families.' Pointing out the value of family allowances, maternity grants, unemployment and sickness benefit, Professor Appleyard concludes: 'Indeed when full account is taken of these differences the twenty-eight per cent difference in average earnings in Australia's favour would be reduced quite substantially.' So there is some disappointment in British hearts. This is complicated by the frustration of the wives whose lives in hostels – if they have to stay there with their small children – are pretty grim and empty. And even when they move into their own houses they miss the warm 'Coronation Street' atmosphere of British neighbourhoods and find the suburban loneliness of a strange land chilly and grim.

All this, one might say, is not Australia's fault. It is bad luck if a new arrival falls ill; the Australian suburbs are what they are and cannot be changed for the convenience of a few British women; and the fact that there is no national health service in Australia is not a closely guarded secret but common knowledge. The migrants, however, say that nothing is common knowledge about a faraway country and when they go for an interview they want to be fully informed. Or to call a spade a spade, they complain of not being given proper and full information in Australia House, in London. Their second complaint is that the Australians fail to prepare adequate accommodation for the migrants.

No one is actually misled in Australia House. What they tell is true; but they do not tell the whole truth. Once I wanted to buy a house near London and having read a delightful description of 'a most desirable property', I drove an hour and a half out into the country to see it. Everything the advertisement said was true to the letter; but it failed to mention that trains ran just at the foot of the garden, almost – one felt – through the bedrooms. British migrants in Australia complain that they find quite a few trains running in their new, beautiful, sunny

'No one is actually misled in Australia House'

Australian gardens. They rightly insist that they are entitled to full information and a proper, un-doctored picture. Mr Edgar Longman, public relations officer of the newly formed United Kingdom Settlers' Association, in a very brief interview mentioned this as one of their main complaints: '. . . intending migrants who go to Australia House in London do not get a completely accurate picture.'

Or take this. Question to a young Scottish technician:[1] 'Could the Australian Government have done more for you as a migrant?' Answer: 'They could tell the bloody truth in the UK about life, prices, hostels etc and not hide the "bad" points.' Some high officials I spoke to admitted that this lack of candour existed, but he added that steps had been taken to remedy the situation.

This lack of 'candour' and of a 'completely accurate picture' refers mostly though not exclusively to housing conditions, the cancerous growth that causes most of the harm in Australian-British relations. One must realise that an assisted British migrant may go to Australia either as a Personally Assisted Migrant or as a Commonwealth Assisted Migrant (i.e. a migrant assisted by the Commonwealth of Australia, not by the British Commonwealth of Nations). The difference is that the former has relations or friends in Australia who guarantee to put him up until he finds his own accommodation, and the latter has no one. This is a tremendous difference. The personally assisted man goes to his brother's, sister's, uncle's or friend's house; the others go to a hostel. And the overwhelming majority go to hostels: about eighty-two per cent of the total. More than a million people – mostly British – have gone through these hostels or are still there. Perhaps I might as well add here that there are a few other categories such as un-assisted migrants, who come under their own steam. When parents and elderly people want to join their families they are allowed in by the Australian government because they find it is much better to let in a few economically useless people than to let a family go home. It is only the hostel-dwellers (who however form the majority of British migrants) who cause the problems.

[1] From James Jupp: *Arrivals and Departures,* Cheshire-Landsdowne, Melbourne.

The position of the Personally Assisted Migrants is blissful compared with the rest. These people, admittedly, often go to the very small house of a rather badly off brother or uncle; perhaps they will be terribly overcrowded for a few months. But everybody can get a good job in Australia, so the new arrivals just save up for the deposit on a house and as soon as the money is in their pocket, they move into their own home. From the moment of their arrival they have also had their brother's help, his local knowledge and the benefit of his experience. Also the inspiration of his example: if he could make it, why not the new arrival?

It is the Commonwealth Assisted Migrant who finds himself in what he regards as a trap. The hostels – and this is a surprise for many – are Nissen huts, temporary contraptions built during the war which ought to have been pulled down years, if not decades, ago, or newly built Malthoid huts, not much better. Intending migrants are told that the hostels are temporary accommodation only and that they can move out whenever they please. But it is not as easy as that. Conditions in hostels vary but it was an Australian Senator, Mr J. P. Ormonde, who described them as 'disgusting and degrading' (*The Australian,* May 23, 1967). The Senator spoke about revolting lavatory conditions and other troubles and went on: 'I think it is disgusting and degrading that decent people have to suffer such privations.' I visited one of these hostels in Canberra – one regarded as the Ritz of all hostels – and while I did not find it either disgusting or degrading, I found even this show-piece pretty awful. Even in the best of hostels the wives, left in the company of small children with nothing to do but to brood over the past and the future, are often heading for a nervous breakdown. In the hostel I talked to Mr James Humpherston – a true Pommy Bastard if there ever was one and proud of it – a former seaman of the Royal Navy, a Birmingham man aged thirty-one, married with two children. He is regarded as a troublemaker because he keeps writing letters to the newspapers and organizes protests, but I found him a courageous and intelligent man, a fine fellow altogether, the salt of the earth. He told me that he had gone through several hostels and had visited many more and the Canberra one was the best; alas, quite exceptional. In others he had gone hungry, partly because the food was not enough and partly because what there was, was uneatable. One of the hostels he had stayed in was situated between an abbatoir and a glue factory. When he complained about various matters, he was called an idiot and he had the strong impression that he had lost his job on at least one occasion because of a letter written to a paper. His boss had nothing to do with hostels but a man who complains instead of putting up with whatever his wise superiors deem to be fit for him, was obviously a dangerous agitator. Various hostel-managers did their best to make his life a misery. Yet, Mr Humpherston remained undaunted: Australia was a fine country, he loved her and had no doubt that he would succeed in the end. Now he had a good job installing oil central heating in private houses, and he would be able to leave the hostel in a year or so. He had no regrets about coming to Australia, he would make the same choice again – it was an admirable country with a great future but he saw no reason whatsoever to shut up when he felt fully justified in opening his mouth and speaking his mind.

Hostel conditions are awful even at their best, and yet this is still not the worst part of the story. People can put up with a lot of hardship as long as it really is temporary. But it is very difficult to get out of a hostel. People can get good jobs in Australia, better ones than in Britain (quite a few of the in-mates of these hostels run their own cars) but they all have to pay for hostel accommodation and the prices have recently been raised rather sharply. One must pay for full board and lodging. One is not allowed to cook in one's own room or cell which is understandable on hygienic grounds; what is less understandable is that if someone has a meal outside, he still has to pay for the meal he did not consume in the hostel. A typical migrant budget: a man – an unskilled labourer – earns £20[1] a week and pays for himself and for his family £15 at the

---

[1] £A1 equals roughly £1 sterling now that the latter is devalued. Two Australian dollars equal £1. Whenever pounds are mentioned, they are Australian pounds, and are therefore now the same as ours.

hostel. After buying a few necessary extras and having allowed his children the luxury of an ice-cream now and then and himself and his wife a visit to the cinema twice a week (one *wants* to escape from the hostel) he is left with a pittance, certainly not enough to save up for a house in the foreseeable future. One needs a deposit for a house. But if one cannot buy a house, one must stay in the hostel. Flats are too expensive and few and far between; rented houses are practically non-existent.

After a period of dark despair, many families decide to throw their hands in and go home. The wife who hitherto stayed in the hostel and minded the children, now leaves them in the care of a nurse (provided by the hostel) and goes out to work. The couple put every penny aside and save up for the journey home. *Why did they not do this in order to save enough for the deposit on a house?* This is a very relevant question and I could find no answer to it. Nor could Professor Appleyard with his vastly superior knowledge. The mystery deepens when one learns that many of these people leave Britain once again and return to Australia, under their own steam this time, and having spent more on the fare than they would have spent on the deposit. This time they work hard, get out of the hostel after a reasonable period into their own house and live happily ever after.

All who survive these harsh months and years become the happy citizens of a happy country. Britons after five to seven years are just, or almost, as well off as native Australians. Some former British immigrants are members of the government – and as someone pointed out: 'no one could tell them apart from the rest'. They have ceased to be Pommy Bastards and have become Right Honourable Gentlemen.

The question that stares one in the face is this: why does the Australian government (with its ex-migrant ministers) allow this hostel situation to continue when it is the source of so much bitterness, bad publicity and – what is more – genuine grievances. A high official explained to me: 'There was a time when housing conditions were quite awful throughout the country. There would have been an outcry if we had cared for immigrants before we cared for our own people. This was a political decision and migrants are a pretty low priority. A politician thinks of voters first; and brand new migrants are non-voters.'

Words of disarming candour. Yet, they are not utterly convincing. Is it really right to induce people in London to come and help build up the nation, and, once they arrive, tell them they are pretty low priority and do not really count? Australian housing conditions improved long ago, yet very little has been done to abolish the 'disgusting and degrading' conditions in the hostels. Here the Australian government, one feels, has blundered badly. Had they put the money they lost on returning migrants into migrant housing, many Britons would be living in much better conditions today; perhaps, as a result of this policy, they would not even be called Pommy Bastards any more, just simply Pommies. To bring out a migrant costs the Australian government a minimum of £ 50. Yet in 1965 140,000 settlers arrived in Australia and 14,000 left permanently: a loss of £2,100,000 and an even costlier blow to immigration policy and prestige. And, as one Briton remarked, if they had added to this fund the money they have wasted on the Sydney Opera, 'we could all live in splendid palaces.'

*　　*　　*

'Are you a Pommy Bastard?' an Australian building-worker asked me when he found me trespassing on his site and discerned from my apologies the faint echo of proper English speech.

This was a new angle. It had never occurred to me that I might be.

'No, I am not,' I answered after some reflection.

No, of course not, come to think of it. I suddenly realized that to be a Pommy Bastard was about the lowest form of human existence. There was only one grade lower: a man, like me, who – all things considered – would *like* to be a Pommy Bastard.

New Australians

On second thoughts, I do not understand how I could have hesitated even for a moment: I could not possibly aspire to the rank and status of a Pommy Bastard. I belong to the riff-raff – i.e. the south and central European mob whom no one wanted to let in to Australia in the first place. The story of the riff-raff, however, is the great success story of Australian immigration, indeed of Australia. Just as British migrants brought a lot of unexpected problems, the riff-raff brought with themselves some unexpected solutions.

Australia's claim to be racially British used to have some foundation in fact: the proportion of people of English, Scottish, Welsh and Irish stock was, before the war, higher than in Britain itself and much higher than in the United States. Today Australia has the highest proportion of overseas-born people of any English-speaking country: about 2,000,000 inhabitants (seventeen per cent) were born outside the country. There are more Greeks than Aborigines, as many Italians as in Trieste or Bari. There are as many Scotsmen as in Aberdeen and as many Englishmen as in Manchester.[1]

Originally no one even contemplated letting in non-British immigrants and contaminating Australia's sacred soil with aliens. Yet the policy had to be changed; paradoxically, not at a time when British migrants were not available but when many thousands of them were queuing up eagerly, hoping to

[1] Data quoted from James Jupp, op. cit. Those who want to explore the fascinating subject of non-British migrants in Australia on an academic level, should study *Overseas Migration to and from Australia*, 1947–1961, a paper by Dr C. A. Price of Canberra University, and also *Australian Immigration*, edited by C. A. Price, Australian National University, 1966, containing a bibliography on the subject.

get in to Australia. The British-Australian immigration agreement was negotiated immediately after the war and put into execution without delay but it became evident in 1947 that there were not enough ships to bring out all the Britons who were eager to come. Secondly, a labour shortage developed in Britain, somewhat unexpectedly, and the British Government refused to raise the number of British emigrants to Australia over 40,000 a year. On the other hand, the International Refugee Organization of the United Nations pressed hard for the admission of 170,000 DPs (Displaced Persons) from Europe. These factory workers, lawyers, accountants, book-keepers, clerks, watchmakers, insurance agents and shoemakers – in most cases former inmates of concentration camps – were, of course, the scum of the earth and not at all welcome. But IRO held two trump-cards: (1) it offered transport, and, for a country in desperate need of immigrants, even a Slovak plumber who can get there is preferable to a true-blue Anglo-Saxon plumber who cannot; and (2) the IRO agreed that the DPs could be directed into jobs for two years – in other words that they could be forced to do dirty work Australians refused to do and to be sent to places at the back of beyond where Australians and British migrants refused to go. After a lot of heart-searching and much against the grain the Australian government swallowed the DPs. This procedure, expressed in proper academic language, reads thus: 'In view of the excess demand for unskilled labour in Australia at that time and the fact that other overseas countries were already accepting displaced persons [what this had to do with Australia is hard to grasp], the Australian government quickly and purposefully made a major change in its traditional policy and agreed to assist non-British displaced persons. Once received, displaced persons were directed into industries and localities for which Australian labour could not be found and to which the government was unable, as there was no provision in its agreement with the United Kingdom government, to direct British immigrants.'[1]

By the time the pool of DPs dried up in 1952, 157,000 of the

[1] R. T. Appleyard, op. cit.

170,000 had reached Australia (against 120,000 assisted migrants from Britain during the same period) and Australia, thoroughly contaminated, felt she might as well resign herself to her fate and let in more of the riff-raff. The Australian Government signed further agreements with Holland, Italy and West Germany, to maintain the flow of immigrants.

As a result of the West-German agreement a large number of SS-men and other ex-Nazis slipped in, to counterbalance the DPs. It was hoped that these countries (plus Britain, of course) would supply enough migrants; but they did not. There was a temporary recession in Australia in the early fifties; Europe, on the other hand, was slowly becoming prosperous and affluent, so fewer people were ready to emigrate, or even if resigned to leaving their home, fewer were ready to go quite as far as Australia. (An Italian from Naples or Calabria preferred to go to booming Milan or rich Switzerland instead of the Snowy Mountains or Kalgoorlie, Western Australia. From Milan or Zürich he could go home to his family for Christmas, an overwhelmingly important consideration for any Italian. A true Neapolitan, of course, detested Milan much more than he detested Queensland or even Kalgoorlie but he was nearer home.) So the search for migrants continued and still goes on – this modern and humane version of the slave raids. Not enough migrants being available from the United Kingdom or, at least, from the more desirable Nordic lands such as Holland and Germany – not enough even from Italy, Greece, Malta and Yugoslavia – the desperate search goes on. *The Age* reported in September 1965: 'To maintain and expand the annual intake,

new areas in Europe, the *United States* [my italics], Turkey and possibly Egypt are under consideration as sources of migrants.' A far cry from the early 'British only' attitude. (The most obvious sources – Asia and Africa – are not being tapped. See next chapter.) According to the most recent available statistics, the proportion of migrants is as follows: U.K. and Dominions 32·4 per cent; Italians, 16·7 per cent; Dutch, 8·8 per cent; Germans, 8·2 per cent; Greeks, 6·4 per cent; Maltese and Yugoslavs, 3.3 per cent each. These are the major groups; Balts, Hungarians, Russians and the inevitable 'others' form groups between 2 and 3 per cent.

This sudden influx of a foreign element could be expected to create tensions and troubles in any country but – in spite of Australia's insularity and complete lack of former mass contact with foreigners – it failed to do so to any great extent. Of course, there was a great deal of prejudice in the early days, hostility and – as I mentioned before – even fights, because Australian youths were annoyed that the young migrants spoke their own language. Prejudice was mutual. If Australians felt perturbed by the influx, resented foreign tongues, feared contamination, were jealous of their women and felt altogether insecure, Europeans often wondered, too: for God's sake, what sort of a country was this and what kind of people? Today Australians are often more broad-minded than the migrants. The Europeans are no longer referred to as *refos* (a nasty abbreviation of *refugee*) but are called 'New Australians', a patronizing but well-meant phrase. Indeed, *New Australian* has come to mean *European*. Little wonder that an Australian traveller came home from his first European trip and reported to his friends with astonishment: 'Funny place, Europe. Chock full of New Australians.'

One often hears about the anxiety of the New Australians that, if a recession comes, they will be the first people to be dismissed. But this is not so certain; they may be judged on their individual merit. In any case, Australia is booming at the moment and the migrants, too, are doing well. Most Australians have one or two New Australian friends: they are more interesting than lap-dogs and cheaper to keep. On the whole Australia has become not only tolerant, but kind and friendly to her new citizens for which the newcomers ought to be grateful.

But not all of them are. It is, indeed, the New Australians who seem to be more critical nowadays. What they like and what they dislike in Australia varies. People from Southern Europe like the economic conditions, good jobs, good pay, house-ownership and security; the English, the Dutch and the West-Germans are impressed less by these factors than by the climate and the wonderful out-door life. People from behind the Iron Curtain appreciate both aspects but enjoy the atmosphere of freedom even more. But most New Australians complain of the prejudices that still survive in many quarters; the Italians dislike the coldness and apparent lack of affection of Australian family life and the easier and more relaxed sexual morality; the Italians also dislike the gambling habits and refuse to buy things on hire-purchase agreements; most Europeans would declare that the average Aussie is content just to work, eat and watch television. Italians, Greeks, Maltese and Portuguese remain more closely knit units within the community, loyal to their national associations and preferring their own national newspapers to the English-language press. They seek one another's company and marry girls of their own nationality. They are often reluctant to apply for naturalization, partly because they feel that whether naturalized or not, they are still regarded as bloody riff-raff, partly to avoid national service. (This second motive has – not unnaturally – irritated Australians, and particularly the Returned Service League, so much that now the migrants are being called up whether naturalized or not.)

People from behind the Iron Curtain – mostly but not exclusively Hungarians – have an entirely different attitude. They are delighted to belong, to be accepted by *someone*; it means a great deal to them to become citizens of a free and prosperous country. They apply for naturalization as soon as possible and become more fervid Australian patriots than the Australians themselves. It was they who resented my critical inquiries most, who tried to sell me cheap propaganda (which they themselves often believed) and occasionally told me downright lies; it was they who informed me that Aborigines did not really exist but in so far as they existed they were all bank-managers or vice-presidents of vast industrial combines. These ardent Aussie patriots adore Australia and yet often do not think much of the Australians. More than once I heard remarks like this: 'I am infinitely grateful to be here. I make a lot of money and like almost everything here, except the natives. They are condescending nowadays and accept us and our friendship but I am not impressed. Most of them are dull, un-educated, narrow-minded and unless you booze with them, you have nothing in common with them.' When I resented this 'long live Australia without the Australians!' attitude, they were taken aback. I pointed out that, after all, it was the Australians and not the refugees who made Australia what it was (although, as we shall see, the ex-refugees make their contribution) and it was the Australians who made it possible for them to live in comfort and happiness. I said I disliked this general dismissal of any group of people and being anti-Australian was not any better than being anti-Semitic, anti-Negro, anti-German or anti-Yugoslav; indeed, coming from them, it was worse. They looked at me in astonishment: whose side was I on, after all? (To be rejected by the Australians because I criticize them and rejected by my fellow-Europeans because I defended the Australians, is a situation which suits me perfectly well.)

* * *

Some problems remain but these may be simply the problems of generations and time may cure them effortlessly. The migrants themselves, it is held, may remain Italians or Greeks, but their Australian-born children will become as Australian as the rest. This is a mistaken belief. Members of this second generation live a double life. At school they are Australians, at home they are Italians (or whatever else they may be). These double standards, instead of solving the conflict, add a new dimension to it. Even people of the third generation are not Australians 'like the rest'; indeed, very often it is the members of the third generation who are engaged in a desperate and intelligent search for their identity: it is they who form national organizations, cultural clubs and become editors of indigenous newspapers.

The migrants' children go to English schools (there are no others in Australia now), they adopt Australian standards in dress, food and work; they become members of the Trade Unions, yet their family values – even after two or three generations – often remain what they were in the home country. They marry girls from their former homelands – or girls of Italian, Greek or Maltese origin – and soccer will probably interest them more than 'football Australian rules' (a kind of rugger, with very few original additions).

An American sociologist, H. G. Duncan found different sequences in his own country. The first generation, although a few of them assimilate completely, adopt only very few American social and economic customs and hardly mix with Americans, and intermarriages are rare. At the same time they cling to their own cultural heritage. 'This stage is essential for immigrant security and happiness' (writes Mr Duncan) 'as too rapid or forceful assimilation causes loss of security, lunacy, suicide, alcoholism and, amongst children, delinquency.' The second generation – called 'the bridge generation' – acts and reacts in the same way as in Australia: preserves the parental culture at home but accepts 'American culture' at school and work, thus acquiring a dual culture of mixed values. Social contact with Americans becomes common and intermarriages more frequent, especially by those reacting against parents who exert too much pressure on their children to preserve the old-world culture. The third generation is called the assimilated generation which completely drops the old-world culture and freely intermixes and intermarries. Mr Duncan is perhaps over-optimistic with this third generation: in America, too, there must be many third-generation people who revolt against pressures exerted by American society and seek some solution and identity in preserving their European heritage.

It was the migrants who popularized soccer in Australia. They established their own sports clubs and the game has become popular enough for Australian television to carry not only local games but – after two or three days' delay – matches played in Britain. Millions watch matches between Bolton Wanderers and Plymouth Argyle with breathless excitement. The migrant teams are resurrections of old Middle-European teams: once again the Hakoah of Vienna fights Ferencváros of Budapest, Polonia meets Pan-Hellenic and the Malta Eagles are at home to Canterbury or Cumberland. Some of the central European matches engender as much heat as they did, once upon a time, in Cracow or Milan. Old feuds are thus carefully preserved, old hatreds and excitements re-lived and fostered: all this has a rejuvenating effect and brings a large piece of central or southern Europe itself to the individual migrant. Australia is a happier land than most others. In no other country could the middle-aged or elderly migrant bring the football ground with him and unpack it with the rest of his belongings.

*　　*　　*

I met a great many Hungarians in Sydney – there are Hungarians everywhere but the Sydney ones are special. There are many well-to-do, indeed rich people among them. I found myself at home in their company, they were kind and hospitable to me and accepted me as a genuine member of the Hungarian Mafia -- which, of course, I was. They have the usual amount of intrigues, jealousies, hatred and gossip in their circle – not more and not less than other human groups need for their survival – but they are a closely knit community. Should their most unpopular, even their most detested member fall upon hard times they will leap to the rescue; they may help him with deep disgust, but they will help him. Hungarians form not only a local clique but also a world-wide conspiracy, third in importance only to homosexuals and Roman Catholics. A homosexual Roman Catholic Hungarian cannot possibly have a worry in the world, he will fall on his feet wherever he may find himself.

They toil, they hurry, they buy and sell, they make money,

they buy houses with breathtaking views and vie with one another as to who can build more modern houses with more miraculous devices and larger and better heated swimming pools.

I found that time has stopped for them: their society is the upper bourgeoisie of Budapest of the thirties, the society I knew so well and which is as extinct as the dodo on the banks of the Danube, but preserved in methylated spirit near Sydney Harbour. Their bridge-parties, their whole form of life, their feuds, their love-affairs, their badinage, even their turn of phrase, all belong to a bygone, almost historic era. You find mummified societies – mummified minor cultures – all over the world: you find Paris of the 1890s in Beirut; Hungarian

provincial life of 1905 in Northern Yugoslavia; Prussia with the Kaiser still on the throne in certain parts of Pennsylvania; turn-of-century Lyons in Canada and so on. It was a pleasant surprise for me to be able to regress in time: to travel 12,000 miles from London and find the Budapest of my youth safely tucked away in a remote corner of the earth.

* * *

Driving through Melbourne I suddenly found myself in Italy. *Mondo Musica* proclaimed one sign, *Salone per Signore* another. Another shop advertised: *Riparazione Electriche*, adding for safety's sake in English: RENT YOUR TV HERE! A newspaper

headline (perhaps a shade too optimistic about our Common
Market prospects) cried out: *Ingelesi in Europa!* Butchers shops
had disappeared and the *Macellaria* reigned supreme. But it was
not only a matter of signs. The streets – usually deserted in
Australia except in the shopping centres, because pedestrians as
a race are slowly dying out – suddenly came to life here, the
streets were full of lively people, gesticulating wildly and
shouting at the top of their voices, simply because no Italian
can speak softly. A little further on I found a Greece as authentic
as the outskirts of Salonika. Little Bourke Street was China, one
of Australia's rather rare Chinese quarters, populated by the
descendants of people who were let in during the time of the
Gold Rush. There are Chinese shops, Chinese inscriptions,
Chinese mah-jong players everywhere, people count on the
abacus and have inscrutable Oriental faces. (Of all the
foreigners, the Chinese have made the greatest contribution:
they have discovered the secret of eternal life. It is said, with
some exaggeration perhaps, that no Chinese ever dies in
Melbourne. When one closes his eyes forever, his papers are
preserved, and his name, his identity, his personality transferred to a mysterious newcomer who has somehow managed
to arrive from South-East Asia.)

* * *

Australians used to find these alien ghettoes worrying, but they
are slowly beginning to understand that assimilation is not the
problem they supposed it to be. Assimilation, to begin with, is
an ugly word and a silly, conceited notion. *Assimilation* simply
means 'becoming similar'; if *you* are to be *assimilated* to *me* the
idea is that *I* am the ideal. If you manage to become as I am,
you are right; if you stay different, there must be something
wrong with you. It is slowly dawning on the more intelligent
sector of Australian society that the outstanding contribution
of the migrants is their very refusal or inability to be assimilated.
To *fit in*, to become an integrated part of a harmonious whole
is one thing; to lose the colour of your personality, to become
just another sheep in the flock, just a cog in the machine, is

quite another. Besides, when assimilation is studied scientifi-
cally, it soon becomes obvious that the term means quite
different things for different groups. For the political scientists,
it is measured not only by the willingness of the newcomer to be
assimilated but by his ability to join political organizations in
the new country; while for the sociologist, assimilation hinges
on the availability of housing, on the existence of indigenous
societies similar to those of the immigrants' and on public
education policy (whether an ethnic group is permitted to
organize its own schools and teach in its own language or not).[1]
Nearly all serious studies point out that assimilation is a two-
sided process: the receiving society must co-operate, not only
by showing goodwill (which often comes and goes in waves:
first, when the immigrants are needed, they are welcome; then
their large number creates resentment and a possible recession
increases this resentment to hostility, till a new boom creates a
more favourable atmosphere once again) but also by creating
the proper social, economic and educational institutions. Thus
the failure of immigrants to be assimilated is not only their
failure; it is also the failure of the receiving country.

The British in Australia swell the number of Australians and
bring with them the same admirable qualities they have always
brought. It is the New Australians, the former Continentals,
who have changed the face of Australia and this has done
Australia no end of good. If these ex-Continentals, south and
central Europeans form their own national associations, let
them; if they keep up their national cultures, Australia will be
enriched by them; if they establish their colourful ghettoes,
Australian towns will be less dreary, less suburban, less
monotonous.

But these migrants have done much more than that. They
have brought a new liveliness to Australia and jazzed up that
happy, rich but rather dull land. A few years ago there was only
one type of bread available in Australian shops, but today all
the world's varieties are there; there used to be only one type of
cheese – mousetrap Cheddar – but today you can get anything
from Camembert to Belpaese and Transylvanian goat-cheese;

[1] C. A. Price (Ed.) op. cit.

the Australian shopkeeper used to sit behind his counter and let his customer serve himself long before the days of proper and organized self-service stores: today he jumps up and serves the customer, who, otherwise, will go to his migrant rival. In restaurants and in Australian homes, chops and peas used to reign supreme; today good French, Italian, Greek and Chinese restaurants are opening one after the other, and Smörgåsbord is as common in Melbourne or Perth as it is in Stockholm. It is the migrants who pulled Australia out of the chop and peas era and pushed her into the age of Boeuf Stroganoff. Today the shops are filled with Continental sausages and delicatessen. A friend told me how when she first went out shopping, she used to point timidly at the mysterious sausages whose names she did not know: 'A quarter of this one . . . half a pound of that please. . . .' It was her hour of triumph when the Continental sausages arrived, and she could ask for them by name while hearing Australian housewives saying timidly and tentatively: 'A quarter of this please . . . half a pound of that. . . .' The New Australians jazzed up business, brought new methods to management, new styles to building. The British migrant remained the solid, reliable raw material; the Europeans became the salt and pepper, the herbs and French dressing to give Australia some taste and individuality. Australia today is simply unrecognizable to anyone who returns after an absence of ten years, and if it is a livelier, more interesting, more go-ahead and more cosmopolitan place, this is largely due to the European migrants.

Assimilation? It is a threat, not a desirable objective. The great virtue of the New Australians is that they cannot, that they will not assimilate. Indeed, if the Old Australians manage to assimilate *to them*, to become more like the riff-raff, Australia might become quite a country. It is more than half-way to that state.

White Australians

Australia has invented a new version of the famous story about the Emperor's clothes. Instead of the little boy looking at the procession and exclaiming: 'The Emperor is naked! He has no clothes on!' Australians exclaim: 'There is no Emperor! It's only his clothes!' This is, at least, their prevalent attitude towards the White Australia policy. Everybody knows it exists; it's not only a 'policy' – it is the law of the land; various people put forward various excuses, apologies or defiant justifications for it. Yet most of them – even those who try to explain it away or justify it – maintain that there is no such thing. The trimmings are there, many signs point to its existence but it is all clothes, there is no Emperor in them. Having firmly established that it does not exist – that any reference to it is a libel on Australia – they will proceed to assure you that this non-existent policy is essential for Australia's defence and will never be given up.

Of all Australian taboos White Australia is the most sacred. Not so very long ago the slogan: 'Australia for the white men!' was openly proclaimed. Today it is not uttered aloud; the very expression 'White Australia' is treated as a dirty word. Not because the practice has really been given up (coloured immigration to Australia is less than a trickle) but because it is extremely embarrassing to discuss it in public.

The 'White Australia policy' is the requirement that only people of European descent – only white people, as some others call them – should be admitted to Australia as settlers. Discussing this question in private, you will find it defended on various levels. The lowest level – and consequently the most often heard

– is this: 'There is no White Australia policy. All we really have is Selective Immigration.'

'But you only select Europeans, never Asians and Africans.'

'Well, they don't qualify.'

There is not one Asian or African, it seems, good enough to be let into Australia.

Then, the same people go on, the non-existent White Australia policy exists only in the interest of Asians, because

(*a*) they would feel very awkward if let in. They would feel different and it is terrible to feel different. So it is better to respect their feelings and keep them out;

(*b*) in any case not every Asian who cares to come could be let in. Even would-be English migrants have to go through a selection process. Naturally, only the best, the most suitable people are admitted. But what would the Filippinos, Indonesians etc feel if the Australians skimmed off the thin layers of their intellectuals, doctors, scientists, technicians?

Well, according to the first argument, the Asians are not good enough to be let in; according to the second, they are too good. Not to mention the fact that a new immigrant feels strange and awkward in *any* country: it's a condition of immigrancy the world over.

During a recent debate in Parliament a member explained that whenever he goes to Asian countries, he never utters the words 'White Australia'. 'I have never experienced any real trouble with our immigration policy when I have visited Asia for the simple reason that I have never in any circumstances used the adjective "white" when referring to our policy' (Sir Wilfrid Kent Hughes in the Debate on Immigration in March, 1966). 'I have never called it "White Australia policy" because it was not so much the policy that caused objection, it was the use of the adjective "white" which implied racial superiority. When that term was used people of other races objected. It was usually the idealists, the do-gooders and, I might say, the left-wingers who went to Asia to cause trouble who stated that the policy was a White Australia policy.' In other words the policy itself caused no difficulties whatsoever; it was only 'I might say, the left-wingers' who caused all the troubles by going to Asia with the express purpose of calling this policy 'white' and stirring up resentment; but Sir Wilfrid, with statesmanlike insight, remedied the matter by never saying 'white'. Another MP explained during the same debate that Australia was a free country, free of intolerance and discrimination. A free country has the right to prescribe who should be let in: this is the way to keep it free. (In other words: keep coloured people out so as to retain your reputation for tolerance. And he is right to a great extent: in a country where there are no black men, black men are not persecuted. That is why so many regard Australia as a haven for white men. Many Rhodesians come here: a blessed country, free of colour problems. But the absence of coloured people does not really mean the absence of the problem.)

It is only the Labour Party which speaks openly of White Australia. Labour, however, under its old leader was a party of orthodox, cloth-cap trade-unionists, sometimes following more reactionary policies than the right-wing of the Liberals. Now, under Labour's new leader, this is changing.

The most important modification of the White Australia policy was when 12,000 Asian students were admitted as temporary residents, under various schemes. These students have always been treated with great courtesy and consideration, not only by other students but by their landladies and everyone else. Perhaps occasional and exceptional slights occur, but I failed to trace one single complaint. In other words, the White Australia policy has managed to lend Australians a worse reputation than they deserve. Most of them, it is clear, are kind-hearted and human on a man-to-man basis: indeed, the Asian students had a less rough time than the European migrants used to have in the fifties. In addition to the students there are another 30,000 Asians, or part-Asians living in Australia either as citizens or as permanent residents. They are all treated decently.

In their most rigid form the discriminatary immigration laws could not be kept up. Occasionally a rich Filippino businessman is denied an entry permit whereupon a terrific uproar follows in the Philippine press – very disagreeable for

Australia, a country which is anxious to prove what a good Asian neighbour she is.

The brief history of White Australia is this: as early as 1837 (less than half a century after Australia was opened up as a convict settlement) the proposal to import Indian indentured labour to New South Wales was rejected on racial grounds. During the Gold Rush so many Chinese (and some other Asians) entered Australia that in 1888 their further entry was restricted by all the states. These state laws became Federal Law in 1901. (One of the reasons for the enactment of these laws, according to Mr Hubert Opperman, Minister for Immigration in a speech delivered in May 1966, was *fear* of economic competition; yet he maintained that in retrospect this legislation was 'courageous and far-sighted. If so, it was the first act of courage inspired by fear.) The 1901 law prohibited the entry of seven classes of persons. The first class consisted of those who failed to pass the 'dictation test'. Although this device was intended to exclude non-Europeans, it led to some amusing results. After World War I, when Egon Erwin Kisch, the brilliant Communist journalist, wanted to visit Australia, the immigration authorities, determined to keep him out, gave him a dictation test in an outlandish language. Kisch failed even to recognize it, and was refused permission to land. He jumped off the boat and broke a leg. He had to be taken to hospital where he spent several weeks. He wrote a biting and witty book on – or rather against – Australia on the basis of his experiences in hospital.

Later there were some slight changes. In 1904 an agreement was concluded with the Government of Japan (and in 1912 with China) permitting the entry of merchants and their families (assistants of businessmen established in Australia). In other words this liberalization was entirely in Australia's own interest. Some students were allowed in, too – a more truly liberal modification. In 1918 Indian residents were allowed to bring in their wives and their minor children. There were further small changes after 1945. Yet Australia's most important trading partner, Japan, was still not satisfied. Japanese concerns insisted on sending more and more people to supervise their interests: furthermore criticism by the outside world – mostly by Asian countries – became disagreeable, so further small concessions were made in 1966. Now, non-Europeans may enter on three grounds: firstly, if they are the spouses or minor children of non-Europeans already residing in Australia (such permits are given now after five instead of fifteen years, as they used to be – an important concession to those already in Australia but as they are few in number, not greatly significant).

Secondly, non-Europeans may apply for entry and their acceptance or rejection will be decided on merit. Not too many have been allowed in and, as a rule, the merit of those who *have* been admitted lay in their being Japanese businessmen. Thirdly, people of mixed descent may also apply and they are on the whole more successful than the first two categories. Although Mr Opperman in his speech of May 1966 – quoted above – mentioned this as a great new achievement, he implied in the same speech that the practice was not new at all but had been going on, in fact, for twenty years. 'In all we would estimate – he said – that over 15,000 [people of mixed descent] have joined us this way *in the past twenty years.*' (My italics.) He also admitted: 'Their becoming part of our community produced few difficulties.'

In other words little has changed in the White Australia policy since 1837. The 1966 law was little more than eye-wash. Even Sir Wilfrid Kent Hughes, hardly a left-wing revolutionary critic of the Government (whose speech I quoted above), talking of these modifications, said: 'Although they may not be very large. . . .' It is characteristic of Australian complacency and self-admiration, that another member (Sir Keith Wilson) should have stated with reference to these not too significant changes: 'I pointed out that following upon the proposed reform Australia now has the most liberal immigration policy of any country.' (With the White Australian policy virtually unchanged.)

Yet the only acceptable and intelligent defence of the White Australia policy is, strangely enough, on racialist grounds. Rightly or wrongly – it has often been explained to me – this policy was followed by earlier generations and as a result Australia is today an almost exclusively white country. Australians mean to keep it that way, simply because they see what is happening elsewhere and they refuse to import a problem, to import trouble and racial riots. They add that a quota system would solve nothing. The admittance of five hundred Indians a year would not alleviate India's overpopulation problem; yet, the Indians multiply so quickly that even such a figure might create a serious Indian minority or an Indian majority in a few decades. (They point to the example of Fiji – of this, more later.)

This argument has some force but it is not altogether convincing and a great many Australians know this. Indians, Indonesians, Filippinos and, from a distance, Chinese, are watching Australia in silence. They do not force the issue at the moment but their steady gaze is a little unsettling. When Australian politicians call the White Australian policy by fancy names and believe that by a mere change of phraseology they have settled everything, they are whistling in the dark. The world is struggling with a stifling overpopulation problem and there is Australia, an underpopulated land, crying out for immigrants but keeping Asians out. Racial policies are untenable in this age. It might be rather dangerous to let the Asians in; it might well prove more dangerous to keep them out.

91

Donald Horne discussing the problem of the coming racial change, remarks: 'It is going to happen one way or the other. It is a task that will be undertaken either by Australians, or by someone else.'[1]

Those millions of silently watching Asians may constitute a future threat; they also give Australia a unique opportunity. Once upon a time, Australians objected to the immigration of Catholics, but Catholics came in and proved to be a great asset to the community. The same thing happened to the Jews; the same to the non-English European migrants: they are proving a great success. There can be no doubt that a reasonable and controlled flow of Chinese, Japanese, Indians and other Asians would do a great deal of good to Australia. Race prejudice is really one of the major idiocies of humanity – simply the fear felt by the weak and insecure. Miscegenation does not necessarily follow from co-existence, but what if it does? There is no special merit in a white skin. It will do the Australians no harm if, in a century or so, they become a little darker. Albanians are not so very much superior to Japanese as all that. This lesson will be learnt sooner or later but a lot of innocent blood will be shed – probably not in Australia – before it is learnt. The mentality of the Alabama sheriff – one of the great intellectual achievements of our civilization – dies hard. Australia could start from scratch; she could regulate the influx and choose the immigrants on merit; she could educate her own people who after a little nervousness, sulking and fighting talk always prove themselves kindhearted and tolerant even to strangers – even if they try to hide it. Australians could live with their new fellow-citizens of Asian descent in the same harmony as they live with their Asian students. Australia, indeed, could be a splendid example to the whole world: an example the world (including Australia) needs badly.

[1] op. cit.

Old Australians

The Aborigines are the black spot on Australia's egalitarian reputation. In Australia all people are equal with the exception of those who are not.

Australia – as I have said – is on the way to becoming a new America. Yet, with all her riches, she has fewer resources than the United States and often has to make do with more frugal means and methods than her great ideal. America, for example, had the Indians *and* the Negroes. In Australia the Aborigines had to serve for both.

The problem of the Aborigines is treated with the usual benevolent 'couldn't-care-less' attitude. Most Australians are not even aware of it. The Aborigines number less than one per cent of the population but they are even less conspicuous than this proportion would warrant if they were evenly dispersed, that is to say if every hundredth person one met or saw were in fact, Aboriginal. Many of them live in large reserves and settlements, in parts of the country where few ever see them. While a small minority of Australians are in constant touch with the Aborigines – or Abos as they are condescendingly called – and like them, ignore them or hate them, according to their temperament and experience, a lot of Australians hardly ever see an Aborigine at all and for the overwhelming majority they certainly do not constitute a 'problem'. As one of the Aboriginal[1] leaders remarked to me: 'For White Australians

---

[1] *Aborigines* is the more usual and colloquial expression; *Aboriginal* is the academic word and regarded as slightly more polite. For me, *Aboriginal* sounds a little artificial; yet *Aborigine* in the singular sounds even worse. So I have mixed the expressions freely, guided mostly by the requirements of euphony.

this is a purely white country; for us it isn't. *They* have no colour problem; *we* have.'

Well-meaning people will explain to you that there are so few Aborigines that the sheer smallness of their number renders the problem insignificant. In 1788 there were about 300,000 of them. (In those days it was, of course, the British and not the Australians who were responsible for the cruelty perpetrated against the native population.) Later the Aborigines dwindled in number to 70,000 but during the war they increased to 100,000. About 40,000 are full Aborigines and 60,000 of mixed race. It is hard to accept the contention that 100,000 people are so few that they are not worth bothering about. It is hard to accept this contention about one single human being.

Others will tell you that the 'Abos' are just a burden on the economy. This is, first of all, untrue, as many of them do useful jobs and are, indeed, respected citizens. But, in any case, what about *their* economy? The white invasion at the end of the 18th century completely destroyed *their* economy – admittedly, a very primitive economy, but their way of life was just as important to them as the white man's economy and way of life are to the white man. 'Economy' in this sense means 'well-being'. Some white Australians regard it as a matter of course that they are entitled to a good and comfortable life because they are 'important' while the Aborigines are not. (I am not arguing for sentimental gibberish about the 'original Australians', about the whole Continent having belonged to them at one time, about their country having been taken by brute force etc. All this is true; but it is also true that all civilized, modern states practically without exception – and most of the uncivilized ones for that matter – gained their territory by conquest, invasion, robbery, destruction and the subjugation of the original inhabitants. This seems to be the general human way, historical etiquette almost. The Aborigines had no chance at all of being luckier than the rest of humanity. Besides, the sentimental approach to any problem is as bad, and often worse, than the callous one. The Aborigines should be treated with due consideration not because they are the 'former owners' but because they are human beings, like the rest of us.)

Other, equally well-meaning, Australians will explain that there used to be a great deal of truth in these charges; but it all belongs to the past. In earlier times, they say, white men – British and Australian white men – committed frightful crimes against the Aborigines and later, for a long time, treated them with ill-will, discrimination and indifference. These times, however, are over. Nowadays Australians do a great deal for the Aborigines and are truly concerned about their fate. This statement is true. An academic gentleman, a great expert on this question and in many matters extremely critical of government policy, told me that now, at last, he thought the Federal Government was doing its best. Yet when one hears these references to 'the past' one thinks of bygone days, of the middle of the nineteenth century or, in the worst case, of the early nineteen hundreds. It is true, of course, that the Indian era – the age of attempted, and in one state successfully completed genocide, passed long ago and was followed by the Negro era, the Age of Segregation (usually referred to euphemistically as the 'age of protection'). It is also true that assimilation became the declared policy in the early nineteen fifties, yet the theoretical acceptance of this policy did not mean the end of the Negro era. Craig McGregor[1] writes: 'In New South Wales and Victoria nearly all discriminatory legislation has disappeared. South Australia made changes in its Aborigines' laws in 1965, Western Australia in 1963 and Queensland in 1965. Even in the Northern Territory Aborigines can now buy liquor, own property, manage their own affairs, own firearms, have access to methylated spirits, sleep with white women (or men), go where they like and qualify for workers' compensation and ordinary social services. It is a measure of the discrimination exercised against them that *they could do none of these things till 1964.*' (My italics).

But even 1964 was not really the date when all *legal* disability ended. The date for this was the May 27, 1967. On that day – I happened to be in Australia – there was a plebiscite and the government's proposal in favour of the Aborigines was carried with a sweeping majority. It was a curious state of affairs which

[1] *Op. cit.*

95

made this plebiscite necessary. Only an estimate could be made of the actual number of Aborigines living in Australia, since they were never counted in any census. Section 127 of the Constitution explicitly forbade this: 'In reckoning the numbers of the people of the Commonwealth, or of a state or other part of the Commonwealth, Aboriginal natives shall not be counted.' They did not matter; they were not regarded as 'people'; not seen as human beings. The law, in addition to being offensive and humiliating, led to absurdities. For a few years Aborigines were allowed to vote in federal elections, yet the constitution did not regard them as 'people'. Further, the Federal Parliament, prior to this plebiscite, had no power to legislate for

Aborigines (only in the Northern Territory were the Aborigines under the care of the Federal Government). The aim of this surprising piece of legislation was simple: it was to leave the Aborigines to the tender mercies of the individual states. Some states were more humane than others. The result of this state of affairs is, that the Aborigines are the only Australians subject to six different sets of laws. An Aboriginal may be almost a free man in one state and a third-class citizen in another.

The six legal systems I mentioned are those of the five Australian states and the Northern Territory (which is not a state). In the sixth state, Tasmania, all the Aborigines were exterminated. The last survivor of the race died in 1869. With his death the Aboriginal 'question' was solved for Tasmania.

*　　*　　*

The law now grants equality to the Aborigines. The plebiscite was an important step in the right direction which, however, means nothing concrete for the time being. This new achievement is not even a promise; only the shadow of a promise. No one says that anything *will* be done; but the plebiscite removes a stigma and, as a result of it, something *might* be done in the future. It should be added that the new, changed attitude and increasing concern of the Federal Government adds an element of hope to this shadowy promise.

The actual situation of the Aborigines is still pitiful. They belong to four main categories. (1) Those still leading a fully nomadic life. Their number is estimated at one hundred by some, at two hundred by others, at five hundred by others again; (2) Aborigines living in reserves and settlements; (3) the fringe dwellers; (4) the town dwellers. In the latter two categories – particularly in the fourth one – there are a fair number of people who live in reasonable circumstances, have their own homes, decent jobs and are accepted members of the community.

In the reserves the Abos are treated well, encouraged to give up their semi-nomadic lives and settle down; they are given medical care when ill, educated in schools, taught hygiene, and given sports and vocational training. Progress is being made; yet, these people are wards of the state and their lives are not the lives of free citizens. But it should be also kept in mind that the authorities, particularly as they have started so late, have an extremely difficult task on hand: to turn semi-nomads into citizens of an urban civilization is no easy matter.

Yes, for many Aborigines the 'full life of a free citizen' offers little. They may be fringe-dwellers, people living on the fringes of small or larger communities. They usually live in huts or shacks made of corrugated iron or cardboard boxes, without electricity and sanitation, in terrible filth and penury. In the cinemas in many townships they must occupy the first four rows, the 'bums' section'. They do the lowest types of jobs and their women often become prostitutes. In some towns they must not enter hotels (pubs) and they are not even served at the back door (whatever the law may say). This, however, does not mean that they cannot obtain liquor; it only means that they have to employ a 'runner', a degraded and depraved Aussie, to buy drinks at the hotel back door. The runner always charges them double or more, yet he is regarded as 'the Abos' only friend'. The town-dwellers find it difficult to get jobs; as a rule they are the last in and the first out; and even when in, they often do not get the rate for the job. The police treat them with suspicion – not always unjustified – and occasionally bully them. One of the Aborigines' leaders told me that a man had been thrown into prison three times because he had insisted – in spite of repeated warnings by the police – on wearing his shirt outside his trousers.

I must repeat that most Australians are not aware of this situation; many others do not care. The 'Abo' is not a feature in most people's lives. When they had a chance of saying something in the plebiscite of May 1967 they uttered a resounding *yes* in their favour. The Aborigines and their leaders were pleased by this but, on the whole, they are still far from satisfied. Indeed, they are bitter and they are watching the Negro riots in the United States with increasing interest. One remembers that the main justification of the White Australia policy was that Australia refuses to import racial troubles. Although the Aborigines are too few in numbers and too badly organized to cause any serious trouble, when one listens to the bitter outbursts of some of the Aboriginal leaders, words of acrimony and hatred, one wonders whether Australia is not on the way to creating her own, home-grown racial problem.

*   *   *

'But for God's sake, what on earth *can* be done for these people?' How often did I hear this question asked, in despair and with impatience.

In private conversations I heard many charges against the Aborigines which are only rarely voiced in public these days.

'They are filthy and uneducated.' Well, many of them are. It is not easy to keep oneself clean on a pittance. Cleanliness is a sign of self-respect; a man whose self-respect is taken away will not be inclined to be clean.

'Even when they have a chance of going to school, they do not learn properly.' Well, some do excellent work; on the other hand, many white pupils are doing pretty badly, too. The Aboriginal child starts off with an awful handicap. His parents, being illiterate and completely uneducated themselves, will not be interested in academic progress and will often oppose a foolish waste of time on studies. Then, it is not easy to do one's homework in a dilapidated and stinking shack, full of quarrelling adults and squabbling children. This is the ancient trick all over again: keep an oppressed minority filthy and then blame them for being filthy; keep them out of the schools, or deprive them of proper facilities for studying, and then blame them for being uneducated. At the time of my visit Australia had one – I repeat, one – Aboriginal university graduate. Some said there was another one. But while everybody could name the one, no one could name the second.

'They do not work hard enough. They do not like working.' Workers of many European nations do not work hard enough, either. Many others – perhaps also the same ones – do not like work for work's sake. A person who feels that he is the last in and first out cannot give his full devotion to his menial job. Loyalty breeds loyalty; indifference breeds indifference. Many Aborigines, who feel secure in their jobs, give excellent service in return.

A further charge is that it is no use helping them. Give an Aboriginal a house and he will still sleep in the open, in his own courtyard. He may chop up his furniture to light a fire on colder nights. All this is true. I myself saw many half-nomadic Aborigines near Alice Springs who were really dirty although they could afford to be much cleaner. I also met a group of artists who were doing a roaring business with the tourists (the son of the famous Albert Namatjira among them), making about £20 a week from their pictures, yet sleeping in ditches by the roadside, and spending a considerable part of their income on taxis. Surely, the authorities have their problems and they too, deserve a great deal of sympathy.

It is also alleged that certain other ingrained habits make the Aborigines unsuitable for the rôle of town-dwellers. Tribal and filial loyalties are too strong. If an Aboriginal earns good money, parents, relations and fellow-tribesmen will descend upon him and take away all he has. He is bound to help them otherwise he will be excommunicated from the tribe. This is quite true; it is also true that we could all learn some filial love and family loyalty from the Aborigines. The upshot of all this is that if an Aboriginal goes to live in a town and wishes to be able to live on his meagre (or not so meagre) earnings he must cut himself off from his tribe – often from his parents too – otherwise he will be bled white. So his will be an extremely difficult decision; he will have to sever all human and family ties and face completely alone a cold, hostile world where he is regarded as a pariah or, in the best case, a second-class citizen.

'They drink too much and cannot carry their liquor', one often hears. White Australians drink too much too, so they should sympathize with this failing. For White Australians, drink is only one joy among many; for the Aboriginal, it is often the only escape from a dreary and painful existence. It seems to be true that they cannot carry their drink and that they become violent or utterly irresponsible under the influence. It may be also true that drink sets free in an Aboriginal such inhibitions, such repressed grief, bitterness and urge to revolt that the tempestuous flood becomes uncontrollable. It may be that if his situation improved, he would have less cause for these periodic expressions and would in turn be better able to carry his drink. Two Australian magistrates have found another remedy for all this: they want to be given the right to whip Aborigines. The two JPs are Mr Ernie Lange, a Pingelly farmer, and Mr Laurie Watson, a Pingelly garage proprietor. Mr Lange said (according to the *Sun-Herald* of May 7, 1967): 'The Aboriginal population has deteriorated since it was allowed to drink just over a year ago. . . . When the Aboriginal drinks he goes off his head. He will do anything. . . . *They would steal soft drinks and sweets – anything.* . . . We would like to order a whipping. It is the only way to stop them.'

*　　*　　*

The most serious of these whispered charges is that the case of the Aborigines is hopeless. They are – I was often told – no good. They are less intelligent than white Australians. They are stone-age people; too old as a race. They are incapable of learning and becoming useful citizens. (The fact that they proved themselves able to learn, given the chance, and that many of them *have* become useful citizens, is, needless to say, not regarded as any argument to the contrary.)

The Aborigines do not belong to any of the three main racial groups but are members of the Australoid race, probably the oldest race of humanity. When they were first discovered by the white men, they belonged to five hundred different tribes and spoke almost as many languages – several hundred of which still survive. A number of early travellers painted unfavourable pictures of them; they were described as a degraded and utterly wretched people who lived on the animal level. The travellers saw no signs of villages, cultivation or organization; and apart from the dingo (dog) the Aborigines had no domestic animals. Their homes were bush-shelters and they wore no clothes. Yet Captain Tench of the First Fleet – who knew them well – described them thus as early as 1793: 'I do not hesitate to declare that the natives of New Holland possess a considerable portion of that acumen, or sharpness of intellect, which bespeaks genius.'

Science has progressed a great deal since 1793. First of all we know that an old race is not a senile race; the life-span of a race does not resemble the life-span of an individual. Further: 'Later investigation,' wrote Sir Julian Huxley[1] 'has conclusively demonstrated . . . that the obvious differences in level of achievement between different people and ethnic groups are primarily cultural, due to differences not in genetic equipment but in historical and environmental opportunity.' He adds, later on: '. . . the frequency curves for two groups overlap almost the whole of their extent, so that approximately half the population of either group is genetically stupider (has a lower genetic IQ) than the genetically more intelligent half of the other. There are thus large differences in genetic mental

[1] *Essays of a Humanist,* Chatto & Windus, 1964, Pelican Books, 1966.

endowment *within* single racial groups, but minimal ones *between* different racial groups.' Clear enough. But a page further down Sir Julian makes it clearer still: ' . . . approximately half of my large ethnic group, however superior its self-image may be, is in point of fact genetically inferior to half of the rival ethnic group with which it happens to be in social or economic competition and which it too often stigmatizes as permanently and inherently lower.' This simply means that half of the Aborigines are genetically more intelligent than the stupider half of the white Australians. Usually it is exactly this stupider half of any population which proclaims racial superiority in the most vociferous terms. It is they who – in this case – insist on depriving the Aborigines of their opportunities, lest the truth come out, and the myth about the stupid man's superiority be blown up. The very suggestion that half of these down-trodden and degraded semi-nomads are genetically more intelligent than half of the white Australian population is repugnant to many. But the truth has never been easy to face.

* * *

Some of the Aborigines get their opportunities and, judging by the intentions of the Federal Government, more and more will do so. The ablest, the most determined and most energetic of them can rise, even today. But this is precisely their most justified complaint. Why only the ablest? As one anonymous but often quoted Aboriginal remarked: 'A blackfeller has to be twice as good as a whitefeller before he's any good at all.'

Strine

When it comes to language, Australians are somewhat resentful or at least silent, about something they should be proud of; and are proud of something about which they might as well remain silent.

Should someone remark that the Australian language, Strine – that's what it sounds like when an Aussie says 'Australian' – is closely related to cockney, Australians are deeply offended. Cockneys, it is true, are even more deeply offended. This mutual touchiness, however, does not alter the truth. Most of the convicts, warders and other early arrivals, who laid the foundations of Australian speech, came from the London area and Essex. There were others, of course, but the London-Essex group was predominant and absorbed the linguistic impact of the others. Welsh, too, had a noticeable influence on Strine for a time but these traces subsequently disappeared.

There are three main reasons why the family likeness to cockney is found objectionable.

(1) Cockney is not deemed to be beautiful. Perhaps it isn't. But Oxford English or BBC-English is not beautiful either. Cockney has no clear vowels, they say. But neither has any other kind of English. Indeed, these slurred vowels constitute one of the major difficulties for the foreign student: he is used to pronounce, say, an *o* as an *o*, without those undertones and vibrations of *u* which every educated Englishman mixes into his *o*s. English is an admirable vehicle for expression: it is concise, lucid and, above all, immensely rich. English is wonderful to write in but it is not a beautiful language to listen to. It cannot hold a candle to French or Spanish, although it is

better than Schweitzer-Deutsch and much better than nasal American. Professor Mitchell has this to say about the beauties or otherwise of Australian speech: 'When an Australian says H-A-Y we say it contains an unpleasant sound. But when someone else says H-I-G-H we say this contains a pure and agreeable sound. But it is the same sound in both.' Mentioning a few more examples, he adds: 'Judgements like this arise from comparisons of dubious validity, and then have claimed for them quite wrongly a musical or aesthetic basis.'[1] Cockney is ungrammatical while Australian, as a rule, is not. Indeed, it would not be unfair to define the Australian language as grammatical cockney.

(2) English, as spoken by the upper middle-class of Britain is regarded as Standard English. But regarded by whom? By the upper middle-class of Britain. Americans and Australians reject this view and are inclined to think it arrogant. English has become the common heritage of many nations and has blossomed in different soils. The English people of England may be the original architects of an impressive structure but many a dilapidated and crumbling cathedral has had to be rebuilt and modernized in later centuries or else they have become just noble ruins. 'Noah Webster,' for instance, writes W. S. Ramson,[2] 'championing the Americans' use of English and looking on British English with the passionate contempt of the reformer, argued that the Americans should not seek uniformity with a corrupt and steadily deteriorating British English.' Webster wrote: 'For America in her infancy to adopt the present maxims of the old world, would be to stamp the wrinkles of decrepit age upon the bloom of youth and to plant the seeds of decay in a vigorous constitution.' These are the wildly extravagant views of a linguistic Yankee nationalist, but language must always remain a living and constantly changing organism. Britain cannot lay down the law for Australian English any more than she can decide what flora and fauna are right – or permissible – for Australia. Just as standard kangaroos cannot survive in

---

[1] A. G. Mitchell: *The Australian Accent,* reprinted from the report of the Australian Humanities Research Council, Adelaide, 1961.

[2] *Australian English,* Australian National University Press, 1966.

Britain, standard English could not possibly survive in Australia.

Australians have never felt superior to American English and have never regarded – as many Englishmen did – original Americanisms as regrettable deviations. As a result, American words and phrases have a widespread use in Australia, enriching Strine. Yet Strine, on the whole, is nearer to British than to American English. Professor Mitchell said he thought that the *Summer of the Seventeenth Doll* succeeded in Britain and failed to succeed in the United States because it was understood in London and was not understood in New York.

(3) But the strongest objection of all is that cockney is the speech of the lower classes. Strine in Australia is not a class-speech; it is universal. In every country – and Australia is no exception – educated people speak differently from uneducated ones, but the slightly cockneyfied undertones are clearly discernible even in the speech of Australian-born university professors from Perth to Sydney and from Darwin to Hobart. In fact, one of the peculiarities of Strine is that this vast continent has failed to produce distinct regional dialects. Some people claim that Sydney English differs from Melbourne English, but this is only because neither city can bear the idea of resemblance to the other; the differences are skin-deep. The truth is that in the linguistically formative years, convicts were pushed around from Sydney to Queensland and down to Tasmania and they spread the same manner of speech everywhere. Later, during the Gold Rush, the population was on the move again, many social layers mixed, a large number of people came in from California and there was a period when there were more Easterners in Western Australia than original settlers. This state of affairs gave little chance to Western Australia of developing its own linguistic identity or even its special dialect. Now, with the impact of television (about 80 per cent of it American material) local dialects have even less of a chance than ever before.

Cockney may not be beautiful, but it is rich, humorous, original and vigorous. Australia has every reason to be satisfied with her linguistic parentage.

D*

Where misplaced pride comes into play, is where Australia's original contribution to the language is concerned. This is regarded as immense; in fact, it is neither immense nor infinitesimal: it is average. Australians show neither more nor less resourcefulness in inventing words and phrases than most other nations. I am only emphasizing this because there is a legend to the contrary. A well-educated gentleman seriously informed me that Australia had a genius for slang and that Australians had enriched the English language by 500,000 original words. Considering that the larger Oxford Dictionary contains 470,000 words altogether, this is quite a claim. (The number of genuine Australian words is estimated by experts at between 1,500 and 2,000.)

Many of these original words are Aboriginal words; quite a few are survivals from the settler days. Words like *jimbangs* and *sollicker* sound magnificent, but the truth is that a considerable proportion of these most exotic words come from that faraway and exotic land, called Britain. *Sollicker* (meaning force) is derived from Yorkshire; *mudfat* from Northern Ireland; *mullock* is recorded in English dialect vocabularies; and *to fossick* (to search) is Cornish. Of the many Aboriginal words, *gilgai, boomerang, woomera, kangaroo, wallaby, potoroo, kookaburra* and *billabong* are just a very few. The desire to live in a town called Wagga Wagga or in a suburb called Woolloomooloo has, on occasions, an almost irresistible fascination for me. *Billabong*, by the way, is the second most popular Australian word. The only trouble with it is that no one really knows what it means. Mr Ramson admits in his book (not in so many words) that he has no idea. The *most* popular Australian word is *dinkum*. 'Fair dinkum' (meaning 'Oh, really?') is reported to be the most often used and most truly Australian phrase. I heard it used only and exclusively by New Australians of short standing who wanted to prove what fine Aussies they had become in no time.

To call a Tasmanian a Tassie, an Australian an Aussie and football footy, is not sparklingly witty. Some phrases are better; others again are very good. The country is the bush and outlaws were the bushrangers; the bush telegraph is the grapevine, the bush lawyer is the man who thinks he is proficient in law, and bush-language is, in fact, not half as obscene as one would imagine. To bush is also a verb; if you get bushed in a big city, you've lost your way. 'She's apples' means that she's all right, quite reliable. If someone goes crook on you, he or she is angry with you or persecutes you. To have a dekko is to have a look out and when you come a gutzer your carefully laid plans fall through. A jackeroo is an apprentice at a sheep-station and if you go home very late, your wife may turn lemony on you. A bird is a sheila and a tough job is a hard yakker. But as I said, no one knows what a billabong is.[1] The trouble is that the best and most original Australian slang is robustly obscene and therefore, alas, unprintable.[2]

I tried to find out what impact New Australians had made on the language, but all the authorities maintain that it is nil or almost nil. This lack of impact is mutual. New Australians made no impact on English; and English made no impact on many New Australians.

A few months ago, two of my ex-Hungarian friends – now living in Australia and full members of the HWC[3] – visited me in London. I drove them around in the country and took them, one day, to the Cotswolds. They went into a village newsagent's to buy cigarettes and picture-postcards and as they seemed to be taking a very long time, I went in after them. The newsagent turned to me and asked:

'You're Australian too?'

'What makes you think so?' I asked.

'You have the same accent as the two other gentlemen.'

---

[1] Stop press news: *a billabong* is a waterhole.
[2] Some of the above examples are taken from *Aussie English* by John O'Grady (Nino Culotta), Ure Smith, 1965; some others from W. S. Ramson's book and a modest two or three come from my own collection.
[3] Hungarian World Conspiracy.

Politics

Australian politicians – and they are not alone in this – protest loudly when they are told that there is very little difference between the Liberals (the Australian version of the Tories) and Labour (the Australian and even less convincing version of Socialism).[1] Harold Wilson has recently dismissed such an accusation as far as he was concerned with ridicule and contempt. Well, it is difficult for any political leader who spends his life in acrimonious battle with his opponents to believe that his opponents are in fact his comrades, while his real opponents, as a rule, are to be found among his own followers. But whatever Mr Wilson may have said, facts remain facts. As any observer can see, the present political era has meant an increase in Harolds and a decrease in ideology. Soon after Harold Macmillan we had Harold Wilson in Britain, and Australia had the late Harold Holt.

Today, it is ideology which seems to be outdated. There is nothing admirable in an ideology *per se*. It depends on the ideology; Nazism, after all, was also an ideology. The world's last true social democratic government was Attlee's government from 1945 up to about 1949. It had a revolutionary programme which it carried out and which was genuinely and whole-

---

[1] Australian Labour spells itself *Labor*. Australia's Socialists, trying to prove that they were a modern, 'with-it' party, looked to the United States – as true Socialists, no doubt, should, considering that the United States is the bulwark and incarnation of modern Capitalism. That's why they chose the American spelling, *Labor*. This, however, is childish nonsense. The word Labour is spelt with a *u* here as well as in Australia, and our Labour Party could not change the rules of spelling by decree. So, however the Australian politicians spell their party's name, I am going to spell it as it ought to be spelt.

heartedly opposed by the Conservatives. What has happened since then? The Tories accepted the Welfare State and the liquidation of the Empire, while Socialists gave up the idea of nationalization for nationalization's sake and the result of this compromise (which happens all over the world) is a *rapprochement* between the parties and the rise of the managers. They have taken over from Moscow to London and from Washington to Canberra. It is still fashionable occasionally to refer to sacred principles and vow that you would rather die than give them up, even if no one – including yourself – has the faintest idea what these noble principles are supposed to be. It is easy to see why the managers have triumphed.

(1) Private property became a major pest and nuisance. People with property became too powerful and ruled too many lives and it became obvious that private property had to be curbed. The question was how one should deal with it. Communism abolished it altogether but the Communist solution failed: workers may be – and indeed, are – just as effectively exploited by the state as by the former shareholders and, at the same time, a great deal of the efficiency of private enterprise was sacrificed. The profit motive, indeed, is creeping back into most of the Communist systems. Britain in 1945 tried a different, more efficient but ideologically less pure method. Private property was allowed to remain in existence – except in certain key industries – but high taxation and the introduction of the Welfare State drew its teeth. (Of course, not enough has been done: much more of the urban building-land should have been nationalized. Land-profiteering and speculation are among the major scandals of our system.)

(2) Anti-shareholder sentiments and the hatred of huge and undeserved private profits was one of the factors which undermined the power of the share-cropper and of private companies and put the large corporation in their place. The large corporation is a new and important development in our life: as a result of its influence we are inclined to make gods of efficiency and management. Governments have not escaped from the impact of this mentality: it often does not matter where one is going, as long as one is travelling smoothly and without jerks. We are

governed by managers, not by visionaries; bombastic rhetoric and fanatical beliefs have yielded to the smooth operator and to the cold fish; and what is worse: to the cold fish with a superior, know-all smile on its face.

Private enterprise and high profits are tolerated in a modern and progressive state only when they go arm-in-arm with high taxation and proper welfare institutions. By these standards Australia is not a particularly progressive state. Taxation is comparatively low and the welfare system is rudimentary. Private profit rules supreme and, in fact, a new-rich class is becoming an extremely influential social layer. (More of this in the next chapter.) Yet, there is something extremely up-to-date in Australia's out-datedness. In similar systems in olden times, the rich were very rich and the poor were very poor. In Australia today the rich are very rich but the poor – by the standards of quite a few less fortunate countries – are also very rich.

This can stand as a fair generalization. But, the truth is that not everybody is well-off in Australia and real hardship exists there, too. Australia has about half a million real poor, over 4 per cent of the population; many old people, some poor neglected children, some innocent victims of crimes, widows, disabled people, a number of not too lucky migrants and a few misfits make up this unhappy lot.[1]

When I asked a well-known member of the Labour Party what exactly the differences were between his party and the Liberals, he reeled off a long list of things. As for example: Labour believes in competition instead of monopoly, that's why they had started a second national airline; the Labour Party would like to see foreign capital controlled – to work in *partnership* with Australian capital – instead of being let in without hindrance, as it is today, with the result that vast sums of money go abroad in the form of dividends. The ALP (Australian Labour Party) is more protectionist than the Liberals: they would like to cut down the import of luxuries; my informant mentioned – with rising passion – that today Australia spent

[1] For detailed information read John Stubbs, *The Hidden People – Poverty in Australia*, Cheshire-Landsdowne, Melbourne, 1966.

large sums on foreign biscuits and $16,000 per annum on imported golf-balls. In housing, he went on, the ALP would like to see a single housing authority and also the end of the housing shortage; they want rent-control and higher old-age pensions. Some of these propositions are pious hopes ('we want to see the end of the housing shortage'; who doesn't?); others the eternal pep-talk of a party in opposition. A party in opposition always wants to raise old-age pensions: when in power they either explain why it is impossible to raise them just now or else do so by a miserable extra pittance. Some other Labour ideas are more substantial but nothing in their programme is revolutionary; in fact, they hardly touch upon essentials. Even if all these ideas are realized: even if Australians have to play only and exclusively with home-produced golf-balls and even if not one single foreign biscuit could be smuggled – let alone imported – into the country, Australia would still not become dangerously red. In fact, it is conceivable, that a Liberal government may carry through most of these propositions.

* * *

Australian political life – like many other things in Australia – is a compromise between British and American ways, leaning, however, heavily towards the British example. The Cabinet system is British. Sitting in Canberra's parliament you might think you were sitting in Westminster. When you are in Canberra, you think that the *general* level of the debate is lower than in Westminster; but returning to Westminster and listening to debates *there,* you have grave doubts on this. The outstanding contributions are, however, much better in Britain. There is one great difference between the two parliamentary systems: in Australia ministers get no advance notice of questions and are expected to answer off the cuff. Answers are more difficult in this system but evasion is much easier. ('I shall look into the matter and shall let the Hon Member know'.) What is non-British in Australia's political life, is that Australia has a written Constitution and that the Federal Parliament is not truly sovereign: quite a few legislative issues are reserved for the states, on whose rights the Federal Government cannot trespass. On the whole, the states resemble the individual states of the United States. (The notorious and backward censorship laws and the occasional but sensational confiscation of books are the work of the individual states.)

The only original Australian contribution to political science or practice lies in their voting system. Voting is compulsory in Australia and defaulters are fined. You must turn up even in order to abstain; or just to spoil your voting paper. One has to give a vote *and also to state one's second preference*. This means that if no candidate gets an absolute majority on the first count, the party at the bottom of the poll loses its votes and the second

preferences indicated on the votes given to this least successful party will be duly distributed among the others. If this still produces no absolute majority, the second last party is similarly treated. Thus it is not possible for a government to come in on a minority vote (as is possible in Britain) and no second ballot is necessary a week later (as in France). It is possible, however, for a party (or person) who was last but one on the first count, to win the election with flying colours, once the second preference votes of the bottom-of-the-pool party are added to its votes. It is also possible for the electorate to express a more efficient protest. In England many people do not vote for the Liberals because they say this would be a 'wasted vote'. This is silly: in this sense all votes not given to the victorious candidate are wasted votes. But this is what democracy is about: wasted votes. In a Fascist or Communist or other one-party state there

are no (or very few) wasted votes. Nevertheless, many people
will prefer to this system the 'wasted vote' idea. It is easier to
vote for a small, struggling party in Australia than in Britain: if
the votes bring in the seemingly hopeless candidate, all is well;
if not, the second-preference-votes are counted and the voter's
wish and alternative preference still weighs in the decision.

The Australian system has, however, one serious drawback:
the power of the donkey-vote is great. The donkey-votes mostly

affect elections for the Senate. The parties instruct their followers: vote for names (say) 7-12, 17-21 and 23-28. But this is
too complicated for many simple souls who just cannot take it
in. So, knowing that they have to vote for fourteen names
altogether, they vote for the first fourteen on the voting paper,
thus distributing their votes fairly and equally among deadly
rivals. Being first on the voting papers for senate elections,
means a great advantage for the lucky party who wins the
draw. In elections for the House of Representatives – where

people are more aware of the candidates' names – the effect is smaller; but in Senate-elections being drawn first means a full five per cent extra votes.

*   *   *

Australia is ruled by a coalition led by the Liberal Party. The disappearance of the colourful, more-British-than-the-British Liberal leader, Sir Robert Menzies, has changed the political landscape considerably. The slightly larger-than-life individual, the orator and old-fashioned patriot has stepped down, and the cool-headed, colourless manager has taken his place. The change is not necessarily for the worse. Individualists, like de Gaulle, are out of place nowadays. Soon after the departure of Menzies, there was also a change in the Labour Party. Arthur Calwell, an old-fashioned, cloth-cap Socialist of the old school (who was in favour of the White Australia policy and supported reactionary Trade Unions in almost everything) gave way to Gough Whitlam, an ambitious, modern intellectual leader of the Gaitskell school. The ALP has been weakened by the change, at least temporarily: loyalties are divided in the party and the new leader has yet to assert his authority. Labour's left wing champions a more radical socialist policy (among other things Australia's withdrawal from Vietnam, where Australian contingents are actually fighting) and they further weaken the party's electoral chances. But Whitlam gains ground, his authority seems to be growing, and the Labour Party seems to be recuperating fast.

The main aim of the Democratic Labour Party is to keep Labour out of office and here second preference votes play a decisive role – so much so that the whole value of these second preference votes is questioned by some Labour supporters. The Democratic Labour Party instructs its followers to give their second preference to the Liberals, so, in effect, the Democratic Labour Party vote – more often than not – means a Liberal vote.

The Liberals live in coalition with the Country Party, a right-wing pressure group of agricultural interests and rich landed gentlemen. Without the Country Party the Liberals would be in a 51–53 minority, but with the nineteen Country Party members, they have a comfortable majority in a House numbering 124 altogether. The Country Party applies its pressure more discreetly and more behind the scenes than Labour's own left wing, so the impression is of greater unity on the right.

I also saw a Communist demonstration on May Day. The demonstrators were led by a band of Scottish pipers whom everybody cheered. No revolutionary mob they. The average age of the demonstrators seemed to be seventeen. One or two people were carrying banners: 'Workers of the World Unite!' 'We Say *No* to Conscription' and 'We Demand a Higher Basic Wage'. There were a few rather gnomic verses, such as:

> 'Die on the job,
> Your compo they rob.'

The not too numerous crowd moved away towards the Yarra River, escorted and protected by police. Both the escort and the protection were unnecessary: they knew their way, they harmed no one and no one meant to harm them. Indeed, few people paid any attention. The whole scene resembled a Butlin Camp do or a jamboree rather than the bloodthirsty march of workers of the world about to unite any moment now.

Should Australia's Labour come to power, it would mean little difference, except to the party leaders and their respective crews. Labour's left wing *would* make some real changes but they have not got a chance. So Australia will go on developing happily as a rich, orderly, efficiently governed and not too exciting democracy where politics is the business of the politicians, and the rest of the population are busy surfing, fishing, driving their Holden cars to beauty-spots and making love when they can spare a little time from making money. This may be dull. But let me mention a few places where life is not dull: Vietnam, the Congo, the Middle East, China. . . .

No Australian Red Guards are fomenting any Revolution, least of all a Cultural Revolution; the thoughts of Chairman Gorton are not being pinned on anyone's lapels. All things considered, I would much rather become a New Australian than a New Chinese.

Snobbery, Australian Style

In the field of snobbery, Australia is an underdeveloped country; even a few British ex-colonies, regarded as underdeveloped in all other respects, could export a great deal of snobbery to Australia and still have enough to spare for their own, internal needs.

This does not mean, of course, that snobbery does not exist in Australia. Snobbery is a common human need, like food or love. It is a by-product of self-esteem. But a lot of people just do not have enough objective reasons to revere themselves ('You have no inferiority complex; you *are* inferior', as the psychiatrist in a memorable New Yorker cartoon said to his patient on the couch). Others revere themselves for the wrong reasons. I knew a famous writer who was inordinately proud of his prowess as a chess-player; I knew one of the world's best photographers who fancied himself as a great thinker and philosopher and inundated me with the trash he wrote; I knew a bio-chemist of world renown and of German origin who never mentioned the Nobel Prize he had received but kept boasting about his English accent which he thought impeccable but which was, in fact, pretty peccable; I knew a successful manufacturer who regarded it as the pinnacle of his achievement that he knew Princess Margaret and her photographer husband. Etcetera, etcetera. Snobbery is a crutch to bolster up our self-esteem: if we cannot revere ourselves for what we are, we must revere ourselves for what we are not. We all need crutches; and the Australians are no exceptions.

But although the rudiments of snobbery are there, its finer developments are basically alien to the Australian soul – that

'*We must be proud of our friends*'

is, if Australians have a soul; many people believe that they are too matter-of-fact and down-to-earth to have such fancy commodities. There are a few titled people in Australia but they mostly have minor titles and no one is impressed by them except the persons who are honoured. When Menzies became a Knight of the Thistle, most Australians were annoyed: they knew nothing of the Thistle and cared less. They felt that Menzies should not have accepted. They did not like the idea that their Mr Menzies should suddenly become Sir Robert and should take it seriously. The monarchy looks remote and unessential, except to the executive members of the Returned Service League and other fossils who are more loyal to the 'Mother Country' than most Englishmen. (I heard of a Dutch migrant who refused to get naturalized. He explained: 'I don't see why, in order to become a good Australian, I should give up my loyalties to the Queen of Holland and swear allegiance to the Queen of England.') Australian papers – to continue the brief list of Australian snobberies – have started so-called society columns but the photographers are always carried away by their healthy instincts and, at parties or at the races, prefer to take pictures of pretty secretaries rather than of homely old Dames of the British Empire.

Of course, there are some hidden corners where people of a twilight world congregate and watch the world go by with stiff upper lips, discussing the good old days when a rich grazier was more than a duke and when all bishops and state-governors were Englishmen. They congregate in the Melbourne and Adelaide clubs or in the seclusion of their palatial houses built on their sheep-stations, are hospitable and quite well-educated, have exquisite, pseudo-English manners and do not really amount to much.

There are two main reasons why the Australians are such poor snobs.

First, they used to be too busy. It must always be kept in mind that Australia's growth is a near miracle; no country has grown, and grown-up, faster in human history. It is less than two centuries ago that the first convicts landed on that vast, unexplored and completely uncivilized island. Rembrandt,

Goya and Velasquez had died long before but there was not a man in Australia who could draw a proper sheep – besides, there were no sheep to draw. In Europe the age of steam was dawning – but there was not one decent lavatory in this new land. The court of Louis XVI was dancing on a volcano, but in the age of Marie Antoinette there was not a single hooped skirt to be found in the whole of Australia. Not that it was badly needed. Australia was short of hard-working men, not of knights bachelor. They wanted people with strong arms not with titled uncles. They needed men who could wield a hatchet and a saw and it did not matter much how they held their knives and forks. Such attitudes – like all attitudes – die hard.

The other reason for Australia's anti-snobbery is this: Australia's second revolution – the Years of Affluence, the Revolution of the Speculators – came just as suddenly as the revolutionary transformation of the land by the pioneers. This second revolution also upset all such snob values as already existed; the country needs time to adjust itself.

Proper snobbery must have a historical basis. In Britain, during the days of the Empire – and it was the greatest Empire the world has ever seen – dukes, earls, royal princes, viceroys and Garter processions served some purpose; today the Empire has gone and all these people and institutions have become relics of a bygone age, traditions without meaning, shells without content. Australian snobbery, such as it is, was always derivative. As long as British power in Australia was a reality, British pomp and circumstance also meant something. In the world of snobbery, prestige and power go hand-in-hand; but Australia is in turmoil today, snob values are all mixed up: those layers of society which have prestige have no power; and those who have power have no prestige.

Why is this? The old-fashioned Britain-worshippers and the graziers do not really count any more – yet they still have a great deal of prestige. Australia's ruling classes no longer rule; Australia's Establishment is disestablished. A new rich class of industrialists, financiers and merchants is growing up fast with all the avidity, energy, imitative eagerness and burning impatience of the new rich. These people are important, they are the ones who count, they wield power – but they have no prestige. They may send their children to the most expensive private schools whereupon the Melbourne 'aristocracy' and the graziers of Queensland sigh deeply and remark that as a result these once famous schools are going to the dogs fast; the new rich may build vast well-heated swimming pools – but vast well-heated swimming pools have come to be regarded as vulgar. (I was one of the minority who regarded a swimming pool as a swimming pool. Not as a status symbol; not as a proof of vulgarity and a cheap mind: but as a place to swim in.)

In Australia British influence remains strong and Australians cannot persuade themselves that 'businessman' is a word that should inspire respect. The United States is not a well-educated country, far from it. But the Cult of the Degree (whether in finite mathematics or ballroom dancing, whether from Princeton or from the most obscure of Nevada's universities) has conquered it. Australia is just waking up to all this. Intellectuals do not count and have little influence; and Degree-Worship is still in its cradle.

The British-type snobs have lost their influence with the decline of British power and the American-type snobs – the snobs of a new and rising world – are not yet safely in the saddle. As the importance of agriculture and wool declines, graziers also decline in importance but they survive as a class. (By the way, you must never refer to a grazier as a farmer. A farmer is a lower type of human. You may call them pastoralists; in fact, a pastoralist is a higher kind of grazier.) They still have vast fortunes and still regard themselves as the aristocracy of Australia, which, in fact, they are, whether this is a compliment or not. They lead secluded and agreeable fishing-shooting-hunting lives, light-years away from the flat-dwellers of Sydney. They play polo, sail their yachts, send their children to Eton and Harrow and mix and marry exclusively among themselves. Some of them never leave their stations, others never go near them; some go up to Sydney once a year (for the Show) and once to Melbourne (for the Cup), otherwise they do not move; others again keep travelling in the grand style – and while their main purpose is still to go 'home' (i.e. to

England which is not their home), they tend these days to visit not only America but South East Asia as well. They have no ambitions left except to lead a pleasant life and go on declining in a most enviable manner. If I had my choice, I'd rather decline with them than prosper with the new rich.

The latter – the bankers, industrialists, merchants and speculators – are the real beneficiaries of the New Gold Rush. They look to Europe and even more to the United States for their values. They regard Australia as a bit of a rough diamond; untrue values – whether spiritual or material – must be imported, not local. I heard of a new-millionaire's daughter who visited her dentist and was told that a tooth had to come out.

'I'll give you a local anaesthetic,' said the dentist.

'Local anaesthetic?' she exclaimed. 'Oh no! Haven't you got an imported one?'

But money, power and even showing-off breeds prestige, so Australia's difficulties in the field of snobbery will be solved. The new rich will sooner or later settle down and will be accepted as a class. The Melbourne and Adelaide club will go on dying for a long time, dying in splendour behind closed doors. (The doors, however, are not as firmly closed as they would wish; more and more financiers and industrialists infiltrate, so the decline of the clubs has become a double decline: a decline in power and in social standing.) The graziers, too, will continue their own delightful and noble decline for even longer. Yet, of course, it is only a question of time until the new rich become the old rich. After all, even the Cecils and the Russells – let alone the Rothschilds and I do not even mention Onassis – were new rich once upon a time. All this granted, I still doubt whether Australia will ever develop into one of the great snobocracies of the world. Australians just do not seem to have it in them. Perhaps they do not as yet revere all the real values sufficiently; but to their great credit, they are not inclined to revere false values either.

3 PLACES

A Tale of Two Cities

Sydneysiders keep on boasting about those very aspects of their city they shouldn't boast about. They stake many claims but you never hear them say how beautiful Sydney is. Sydney is, in fact, one of the most beautifully situated cities in the world, not forgetting Rio de Janeiro or Istanbul. There are few sights on this globe to rival Sydney Harbour with the lovely bays and beaches in the distance, and majestic Sydney Harbour Bridge, its single arch of 1650 feet (2¼ miles with the approaches)

connecting Sydney (i.e. the City) with its northern suburbs; the fast developing and rapidly changing sky-line has grown up so quickly that people have hardly had time to get used to it.

People in Sydney keep talking about the *view*. Everybody must have a view, and everybody's view (in new rich circles) must be better than everybody else's. The view, in fact, is second only in importance to a large, heated swimming pool. Here the reader may remark that I am talking nonsense: how can I say that Sydneysiders are not proud of the beauty of their city if they keep boasting about the view? Surely, the very idea of the view implies that the people of Sydney know that they have something worthwhile to look at? True enough; but there is a difference here. The view is something personal and private; it is *your own personal view;* it is – for them – the beauty of their house or flat and not Sydney's. Sydney with its bays, beaches and bridge, is just the background; the view is an integral part of the house itself.

I have seen many of these views and, let me repeat, the panorama is breathtakingly beautiful. First Prize for the best view goes – without hesitation – to the Gents in the American Club. (Which shows that women are still denied equal rights in Australia.)

Sydney is the largest city in the country but Melbourne, its great rival, is a close runner-up. As usual in such cases, the eight sets of statistics I looked up give eight different figures for the respective populations. Calculations based on the available evidence seem to show that Sydney has about two and a quarter million inhabitants, Melbourne just over two million. Close enough, one may say; not much in it. Sydney keeps referring to itself as 'Australia's largest city'. As Melbourne does not contest the claim, we may rest assured that Sydney *is* Australia's largest city. But while Melbourne does not contest the claim, neither does it confirm it. You will never see a reference in Melbourne to itself, as 'Australia's second largest city'. No fear. In the pamphlets and other literature I picked up in Melbourne, the reference is usually to 'one of Australia's two largest cities'. It should also be noted that Sydney and Melbourne, between them, account for more than one third of the country's population; the six state capitals together account for more than half.

Sydney is very Australian: it has an individuality and identity of its own; and it is also very European; and cosmopolitan. It bustles; it hurries; it is alive. All this makes Sydney a very attractive place. But the city itself has few actual points of attraction, few places of real interest and practically no history. A little official map gives the car park sixth place among 'Some

Places of Interest', coming after the AMP Building, a government office block, the Art Gallery, the Botanic Gardens and the Building Information Centre. Now, the government office block – on the corner of Macquarie Street and Bent Street – may be a matter of taste; the Building Information Centre may fascinate some more than others; but few people will travel really far to see a car park. (Well, of course, many people often do travel quite far to see a car park; but I mean: to see a car park exclusively for its beauty.)

As you walk around in Sydney and around Sydney you can hardly fail to notice how derivative most of the names are. Many echo London: Hyde Park, Bayswater, Paddington, Kensington, Kings Cross; many others are aboriginal: Narrabeen, Coogee, Wattamolla, Parramatta, Wollongong, Ku-Ring-Gai; some are Continental: one of Sydney's suburbs – surprisingly – is called Vaucluse; and the few original names are, as a rule, not too imaginative: Freshwater, Whale Beach, Dawes Point, Millers Point.

Before arriving in Australia I had heard a lot about Sydney's hotels and about Australian pubs in general. These pubs have quite a literature and folklore; they are legendary. You are told that you can meet the 'people' there; that conversation is wonderfully relaxed and original, and that everybody is kind and friendly. I found people in the pubs kind and friendly indeed but neither kinder nor friendlier than outside the pubs. I heard but few scintillating remarks and not one unforgettable aphorism on life in general. Some people were only too keen on uttering trivialities and clichés but most of them remained silent and regarded a man with an Anglo-Continental accent with slight but ill-concealed disgust. At frequent intervals newsvendors entered with new editions of the afternoon papers, containing the latest racing results. Everybody bought a paper except me, which confirmed people's suspicions about me. On such occasions the hush of a Turkish bath – which had reigned up to then – was replaced by the stillness and tranquillity of a village cemetery, interrupted only by the rustling of the pages and by an odd sigh of resignation or despair now and then. In an Australian pub men just stand around the counter – in strict segregation, women are not tolerated except in back-rooms – and drink beer; that's all. I am ready to concede that this is not unnatural for a pub; on the other hand there is nothing much in it to admire.

Another famous and much praised spot of Sydney – the heart of the city, its pride, the final proof of its cosmopolitan character – is Kings Cross. It is not as Londoners might conclude, a railway station, but Piccadilly Circus, swinging Chelsea, depraved Soho and restaurant-Soho all rolled into one. Sydney, I must repeat, *is* a thrilling, cosmopolitan city with an ambience of its own; but I was no luckier with Kings Cross than I had been with the pubs. The place, it is true, does come up to its reputation as a restaurant district. In Sydney (and also in Melbourne) you can find as many delightful restaurants as in London (the last named being another town which, in the last ten years, has turned itself from one of the world's most awful eating places into one of the best). But what else is there at Kings Cross? I visited the place with great expectations, hoping to find gaiety and noise and just enough sin to stir up a teeny-weeny spark of moral indignation in my bosom and make me feel righteous. But Kings Cross is no den of iniquity. Perhaps I visited it on the wrong day but anyway I did find it completely lifeless. All I saw was a few American tourists in search of reverberating laughter, sin and rebellious youth. They searched in vain; the place was half-asleep. Kings Cross must be Billy Graham's delight: the most virtuous brothel-district in the world. A solitary, bearded man came along, bare-footed. He looked lonely and sad. He looked like a man carrying out an unpalatable duty: keeping up the reputation for oddity and eccentricity of a place in which he himself had long ceased to believe. I liked him: he looked a dedicated man doing a distasteful job conscientiously.

I went into a striptease joint, too. Hefty Australian girls glowing with rude health were going through motions which looked like dancing. Towards the end of the dance they bared their bosoms which made them look more than ever like advertisements for some health food rather than sirens and odalisques. A vicarage tea party seemed to be a sexy and erotic occasion compared with this. The place was sober, respectable and strictly unlicensed. The hefty nudes had to be enjoyed with a lemonade in hand – a drink perfectly suited to the occasion.

*　　*　　*

In the thirties, when the Jews of Europe, threatened by Hitler, were searching for places to emigrate to, there was a popular joke about Australia. One would-be-emigrant tells another would-be emigrant he has decided where to go: to Australia. The other wrinkles his nose and remarks that this is an odd choice as Australia has no culture and no opera. The first man gets angry: 'Tell me, how many times have you been to the opera in the last ten years?' The other replies: 'Not once. But the knowledge that the opera is there. . . .'

Apparently it was this omission that Sydney set about to remedy when it decided to build an Opera House. The operation has become one of the great building scandals of the age. The story is well known, so I shall give here only the gist of it. A Danish architect, Joern Utzon, having won the competition was entrusted with the job of building the Opera House, which the Government expected to cost £3 million. The rest is simply a tale of lack of communication between bureaucrats and artists. The bureaucrats and politicians – first of all the Minister of Public Works of the New South Wales government – were taken aback to find that instead of £3 million they were expected to cough up more than £30 million, and even so no one could tell for sure when the first opera would be sung in the building, or, indeed, how much more money would be needed. To which Utzon and his fellow-artists replied that the new opera house was to be a work of genius (which is absolutely true), not only *the* most beautiful and original building of this half-century – perhaps the whole century – but also an experimental structure; and no one can budget for something no one else has ever done or attempted before; this was no office block, after all. The minister was reduced to tears. He tried to explain that a budget was a budget and no Treasury likes to be told that a building is to cost ten times – perhaps twenty times – as much as anticipated. Words like 'beauty' and 'inspiration' and 'poetic lines' have no place in budget speeches. The argument became embittered: Utzon was accused of amateurishness, unnecessary delays, wrong organizational approach, reckless spending etc; his colleagues countered with charges of lack of understanding, of petit-bourgeois small-mindedness, obstructionism, bureaucratic bungling. Utzon was dismissed and replaced by a committee; he sued his former employers for breach of contract and things went from bad to worse. Costs went on swelling in the meantime but this didn't matter because the Opera was financed by a lottery. The lottery – with frequent draws – brings in money galore, so the Opera House is no burden on the tax-payer.

The outside of the Opera House is completed; the building is near the harbour and looks like a huge, graceful sailing boat about to cross the infinite waters. It is one of the most beautiful and romantic buildings in the world. The inside it seems will not quite match the outside. This is now in the hands of a committee of architects who are not – cannot be – as good as Utzon was. Their first move was to change the Opera into a Concert Hall only, and try to cram opera-production into a small theatre hall. I went to see the building and whatever the outcome of the lawsuit, it will remain Utzon's creation. In a decade or two few people will remember who the Minister of Public Works of New South Wales was who built the Opera; but everyone will know the name of the architect who, unfortunately did not quite build it.

In the meantime, the Sydney Opera is becoming the world's most famous opera house. People talk more of the Sydney Opera than of the Metropolitan and La Scala, Milan, put together. It will be almost a pity to finish it; but luckily the danger of that seems to be remote.

But this is cold comfort: now Melbourne is threatening to build its own opera house and have it ready first.

*　　*　　*

The rivalry between Sydney and Melbourne is keener than any other rivalry in Australia. In other cases the rivalry is between states; in this case it is between cities. All the same, in this case too the fact that Victoria used to be part of New South Wales must have something to do with it. The second city grew and grew and its people were dissatisfied with the New South Wales government; in addition, Sydney, they felt, was too far away. They decided to form their own state but the New South Wales government would not even listen to such a proposition. Then a small group of citizens had the idea of petitioning the Queen herself. The petition was couched in more human than political terms and every line of it radiated loyalty to the Crown and devotion to the Queen, so the Queen was moved and allowed them to secede. In gratitude the new state was named after her; its capital bears the name of her Prime Minister. So Victoria is the prodigal daughter, determined to show her parent that she has made good; Sydney is the smug father, determined not to be impressed.

New South Wales is not the largest of the Australian states but the oldest, the most populated and the most industrialized. Victoria is the smallest of the mainland states but second only to New South Wales in population and industrialization. New South Wales also contains Australia's highest mountain peak, Mount Kosciusko, 7,328 feet. It is quite a feat to climb it; it is also quite a feat to pronounce its name – why *should* anyone know how to utter the name of this once famous Polish revolutionary who defied the Czar? – and most Australians give up both attempts; Kosciusko, when mentioned, usually becomes Kozy. Around it, in the Snowy Mountains, they are building a gigantic hydro-electric plant which – needless to add – is the largest in the Southern Hemisphere. For anyone interested in hydro-electric plants the place is of absorbing interest. The Snowy Mountains are developing into a wonderful ski-ing area and ski-ing is rapidly becoming the great in-sport of Australia. New hotels and ski-lifts are going up everywhere and the facilities will soon rival Switzerland. A couple from Sydney or Melbourne might leave on the same day for their holiday: the wife might go sun-bathing at Surfers Paradise, in Queensland, the husband ski-ing in the Snowy Mountains. A lucky country.

The great difference between Victoria and New South Wales,

the dividing line between two civilizations is that while in New South Wales one-armed bandits are permitted, in Victoria they are banned; and an even more important difference: in Victoria they play – in fact they are mad about – football (Australian style) while in New South Wales, somewhat predictably, they regard it as a childish pastime. Australian football, as I mentioned earlier, is neither Australian, nor football. It is rugger played with slight changes, with a slight Australian accent. (It differs less from rugger than baseball differs from cricket or than American football differs from soccer.) Victoria is altogether more Victorian: strict, puritanic drinking laws have been only very recently abrogated and the censorship of books is about as vicious as in Ireland. Not only *Lady Chatterley's Lover* but also *The Group* is banned. In fact, Victorian censorship is more backward than the Irish: the police make more of a nuisance of themselves and booksellers cannot even get a list of banned books. Of course, these oppressive police methods also have their good side. For an English publisher it is not quite so good to be banned in Victoria as it is for an American to be banned in Boston, but it helps.

But – for me – the most interesting places of the two states remain the large and impressive cities. Melbourne has less rain (which means in Sydney language that it is parched); Sydney has more sunshine (which means in Melbourne language that Sydney is a place of tropical heat); Melbourne gets cooler earlier in the year (which, for Sydney, means that Melbourne has an arctic climate).

Melbourne has no harbour bridge and no views comparable with Sydney, but it has the pretty Yarra River, some nice enough views and, on the whole, is the more attractive and better built city of the two. It has a more sedate and dignified atmosphere (which for Sydney means that the place is a deadly bore and half dead); Sydney is more lively and awake (which for Melbourne means that it is noisy and vulgar). If Melbourne has no harbour bridge, it has the Melbourne Cup which few Melbournites would exchange for any bridge in the world. This is Australia's greatest horse-race, run on the first Tuesday of November. But it is more than a simple horse-race, it is a

E

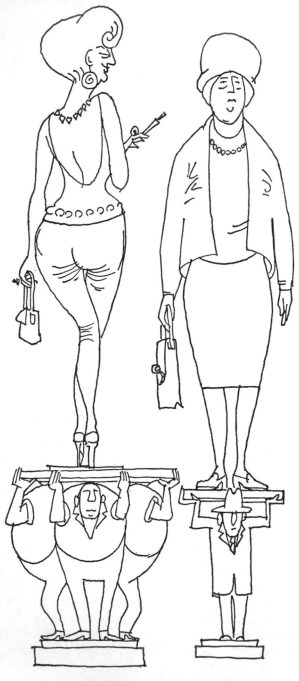

'*Melbourne has no harbour-bridge*'

national event and it is no exaggeration to say that the Cup has played as important a part in the growth and development of Melbourne as the Harbour Bridge in that of Sydney. Melbourne is Australia's financial capital; and it is not the Americanized new rich who set the tone but the English-type and English-educated upper middle class, the bankers and professional people. Yet, conceding these differences, I am going to say something sacrilegious: there is really not all that much difference between the two cities.

Melbourne, it is true, is the more artistic and more intellectual of the two, which means that it is the most artistic and most intellectual city in Australia. It has the best art gallery, some of Australia's best painters are Melbournites and so were two recent Prime Ministers, Menzies and Holt. Political discussions are livelier there than in Sydney (after all, Melbourne used to be the nation's capital), it has more parks than Sydney and Toorak is regarded as a more exclusive suburb than anything Sydney – or the rest of Australia – can boast of. All these points are granted. The inhabitants may feel very strongly about these points of difference, just as the English and the Scots do. But for the outsider the English and the Scots, while they possess some noticeably different traits, are people belonging to the same civilization, with the same manners, mannerisms, peculiarities, sense of humour, outlook and attitudes towards the rest of the world. Similarly, to my non-Australian eyes, the differences between Melbournites and Sydneyans while real are certainly much smaller than, say, between northern and southern Italians or between French-speaking and German-speaking Swiss. I know that after this statement I can never again show up either in Melbourne or in Sydney but let me repeat it in my true indomitable spirit: Melbourne is rather like Sydney; Sydney is rather like Melbourne.

Canberra

Canberra, the national capital, is the least Australian of all Australian cities. The very idea of having a city especially built as a capital, far removed from all the other big centres, is an

American invention. Such a capital – this is the basic idea – is uninfluenced by commercial, financial and industrial pressures; but it is also uninfluenced by life itself. It is an artificial flower, a community inhabited by politicians, civil servants and

diplomats who know what is happening in their own, hermetically sealed circles, but are always a little behind the times as far as the outside world and public opinion are concerned. Canberra is much better than Washington: it is less isolated, less inbred, less preoccupied with itself. It also helps that while it is the centre of administration and government, it is not the centre of real power: the important decisions are made elsewhere. Canberra is less formal, less pompous, less class-ridden than Washington (although these vices seem to be creeping in, as Canberra grows in size and importance). In the lunch-interval, many civil servants change into purple, red and green sporting attire and play cricket or football. Inter-departmental matches are fought out with great zest and watched by enthusiastic colleagues as well as by benevolent, elderly superiors.

Luckily, Canberra is also an important seat of learning: the Australian National University is there as well as the School of Medical Research and, just outside of Canberra, in Tidbinbilla and Orroral, is the site of an Australian-American outer-space tracking station.

There are further important points of difference between Canberra and other Australian cities. Other cities grew like wild flowers, Canberra, to its great advantage, was planned. It was an American, Walter Burley Griffin, who planned it and he obviously had Washington in mind. Canberra, too, is a garden city, with spacious, wide boulevards and lovely parks and its main streets radiate from a centre (in fact, from two centres: City Hall and Capitol Hill).

Other cities are busy making money, Canberra is busy spending it. This is no criticism or jibe, it is a word of praise. Spending money is a more leisurely, gentlemanly and agreeable occupation than making it and Canberra is, consequently, a more leisurely, gentlemanly and agreeable place than the breathless money-making centres.

All the other Australian capitals are on the coast, Canberra is an inland city. (Most Australians reading this sentence will raise an eyebrow. When 'capitals' are mentioned they have state-capitals in mind and Canberra is not a state capital. As

Washington is called 'DC' – District of Columbia – Canberra is Australian Capital Territory, a little above and a little below the states. But as, after all, Canberra *is* the Federal Capital, I may be forgiven for calling it a capital.) Well then: all the other capitals are on the sea-side, Canberra is on the shores of a lake. Not that Canberra was built on the shores of a lake; a lake was built around Canberra.

*   *   *

Perhaps before explaining how the lake came to Canberra, I might as well describe briefly how Canberra itself came into existence and why it is where it actually is. The six former Australian colonies – the ancestors of the present states – came to realize early that close co-operation, perhaps even federation, would be to their advantage. Intercolonial conferences were held at irregular intervals from 1863 onwards. One of these conferences was held in 1891, under the sponsorship of Henry Parkes, Premier of New South Wales. This conference – or rather convention – drew up a draft Federal Constitution and, on its basis, the Commonwealth of Australia came into being on January 1, 1901: so federal Australia is as old as the century (which did *not* begin on January 1, 1900 as most people believe and as, perhaps, it ought to have done). The first Parliament in Australia was opened by the future King George V; the first Parliament in Canberra by his son, the future King George VI, twenty-seven years later.

One question, among the many which the Federal Constitution had to settle, was the location of the capital of the new Commonwealth. They chose the American solution not because it was so good but because neither Sydney nor Melbourne would accept the other as capital. Their struggle ended in a complicated compromise: Sydney achieved its wish that the new Capital Territory should be carved out of New South Wales but had to agree that it must not be nearer to Sydney than one hundred miles. In return, Sydney had to agree that Melbourne should become the temporary capital – to which it probably would not have agreed, had it then been known how long this 'temporary' period would be. Melbourne housed the Federal Parliament for more than a quarter of a century.

The search for a site for the new capital started immediately. Many sites were suggested and inspected; the issue was bitterly contested but, in the end, they selected the most obvious spot: a site between Sydney and Melbourne, on the straight line connecting the two rival giants, well over a hundred miles south-west of Sydney and about twice as far north-east of Melbourne. The selection of this obvious site took ten years.

Why is the Commonwealth of Australia called a Commonwealth and why is the capital called Canberra? The name of Commonwealth was suggested by Parkes and most eloquently advocated by an academic friend of his called Barton. 'Commonwealth,' Mr Barton said, 'is the grandest and most stately name by which a great association of self-governing people can be characterized.' We all know, at least, where the expression 'Commonwealth' originates from; but no one really knows where the word Canberra comes from and what it means. It is known, of course, that the site ultimately chosen for the Federal Capital was the district of Yass-Canberra but this tells us nothing of the etymology. It is almost certain that this euphonious Latin-sounding word – which could be the name of an Italian province or a melodious Spanish swear-word – is, in fact, of Aboriginal origin.

*   *   *

Canberra is a success-story but it started off as a failure-story *par excellence*.

When I visited Rio de Janeiro a few years ago, one of the European ambassadors invited me to lunch. My host was a little late; on arriving, he explained that he had had to call on the Foreign Minister that morning. The President of Brazil had made it an absolute rule that foreign diplomats were to be received by the Foreign Minister in Brasilia only – another artificial capital, then brand new. So my host had to take the early morning plane from Rio to Brasilia, and could not fail to notice that the Foreign Minister was on the same plane. In

Brasilia the two men discussed their business and then took the same plane back to Rio. So they travelled about 1,400 miles to have a chat with each other; starting off from the same city and returning there as soon as possible. 'But one day you will have to move to Brasilia and live there,' I told my host. He replied with a slightly malicious grin: 'It is my successor who will have this pleasure.'

Brasilia has gained ground since those days; but for a long time Canberra was no more popular than Brasilia in the days of my visit. Canberra was a dreary village containing a few large, impressive and very un-village-like buildings. For a long time it had only 5,000 inhabitants. Canberra began to develop slowly, very slowly, and its development received three successive blows – almost knock-out blows: the two world wars and the depression of the thirties. It looked as if it could never recover and never become a city of any size and importance, let alone the true capital of the Commonwealth.

But in 1958 a miraculous development set in and Canberra has never looked back. Its development is staggering. Many people told me that Canberra was the fastest-growing city (guess where) in the Southern Hemisphere; a few others staked an even higher claim, stating that it was the fastest-growing city in the English-speaking world. The evidence of my own eyes was so impressive that I was inclined to accept both of these statements until I read the following sentence in one of Craig McGregor's books: 'Elizabeth is the fastest-growing community in Australia.'

Whichever is the record holder, Canberra soon found that it needed some water to increase its beauty. Griffin, the American architect who had first planned Canberra had planned a site for a lake too; the site was there but no lake, now everything was prepared in advance, even a bridge was built over the non-existent lake. Eventually the water – borrowed from the nearby river – was gradually let in: it took a few months to fill the lake but by now it had become a most impressive sight and there is nothing artificial-looking about it. It is called Lake Griffin, after the American architect. He never quite finished his work. He departed after a quarrel (like

136

Utzon, the planner of the Sydney Opera House) but the lake is, nevertheless, named after him and not after the Minister of Public Works. The lake *makes* Canberra; it is beautiful, blue and majestic. Some people say that the old meadows, with cows grazing where the lake is now, were prettier but this is just prejudice and hankering after the good old days. Whatever else the brand new lake (it arrived in the early sixties) did to Canberra, it certainly upset all the old snob-values. In the pre-lake era one had to live in the north side, the south was just not fit for a gentleman. Today everybody must have a view of the lake and the formerly despised south – now the southern shore of the lake – is one of the most sought-after and expensive parts of a very expensive city.

*　　*　　*

So the former inland village of 5,000 people became a beautiful, busy, lake-side city of about 100,000 inhabitants. By the nineteen eighties Canberra will have a quarter of a million people. Building operations are going on at feverish speed; you can almost *hear* the place grow. What is more, the once despised provincial hole – the mere compromise in the Sydney-Melbourne jealousy – has become Australia's true and recognized Capital City (the tenth largest city in the land) of which Australians are justly proud. About half a million tourists (mostly Australians) come to admire it every year. (London, at the same rate, ought to have forty-two million visitors per annum.)

Statistics impressed me on this particular occasion, but a remark I heard brought home to me Canberra's fabulous growth more than any figures. My car was just passing a fine big school with hundreds of happy sun-tanned children playing about outside it. The paint was hardly dry on the walls. I asked my guide:

'Is this a new school?'

He shook his head firmly.

'God, no. It's last year's.'

Hobart

The outside world knows little about Tasmania's own royal family and today most Tasmanians regard it as a bit of a joke; nevertheless, this royal family exists. Tasmania, once upon a time, toyed with the idea of seceding from Australia and establishing a new monarchy. No foreign prince was to be invited to the Tasmanian throne: no Hohenzollern or Hohenstauffen, no Bourbon and not even a Hanoverian: if Tasmania was to have a king, she was to have her own, indigenous royal house. The royal family was in fact designated, even if very unofficially. The King of Tasmania was never crowned, but the family is still known and respected; its senior male representative enjoys the aura surrounding all pretenders (although he does very little active pretending nowadays). Perhaps there are a few people who think that – with Britain becoming more and more remote – he still has a chance, but this is not the real reason for the survival of the legend. As one Tasmanian royalist explained to me: 'It's good for tourism.'

Tasmania, of course, gave up any idea of seceding from Australia; perhaps because it has, in fact, seceded. It did not secede politically: it is one of the six states of the Commonwealth of Australia even if many Australians, visiting Tasmania, wrongly believe that they need a passport (they do, after all need a passport *and* a permit when visiting that northern island, Papua-New Guinea). Tasmania seceded first of all geologically. The Bass Strait did not always exist and cannot, in fact, be more than a few hundred million years old, if that – a span of time of which geologists always speak with contempt as if it were hardly worth mentioning. And after that Tasmania seceded psychologically, which is even more important. A Tasmanian is not an Australian; he is a Tasmanian, just as a Yorkshireman is a Yorkshireman. But as the Tasmanian is, politically at least, also an Australian (just as the poor York-shireman cannot help being British) he cannot refer to other Australians as Australians. Instead he defines them as *Main-landers*. Mainlanders – and let there be no mistake about it – is a term of contempt; when the word is uttered, or spat out, by a genuine, proud Tasmanian, it sounds as though the mainland was a small and not too important annex of Tasmania. Main-landers are not called migrants as yet, but they are thought of rather as New Australians. Migrants, in fact, are held in slightly higher esteem than Mainlanders. A foreigner true and proper – a Hungarian or a Maltese, even a Briton – has a better chance of being accepted than a man from Adelaide or Wollongong. A Mainlander has to prove himself, to work his way up; he has to make good, in fact.

The Tasmanian-Australian relationship is a replica of the Australian-British relationship. Australia is now a rapidly developing, rich and modern place but used to be, for long, very much the provincial continent; it was also suspicious of Britain and resented being treated as the distant, provincial nephew. Similarly, Tasmania refuses to play the part of the poor colonial *vis-à-vis* Australia. Tasmania is sixty times nearer to Australia than Australia is to Britain (about 200 miles against 12,000) but distance is not only physical. Tasmanians dislike Mainlanders partly because Tasmania is an island and islanders tend to be smug and self-satisfied (the people of Ibiza look down upon the rest of Spain, just as Greek Cypriots look down upon the rest of Greece or – to mention another southern island at the tip of a continent or sub-continent – Ceylonese regard themselves as superior to Indians). But Tasmanians do not think much of the Mainlanders for another reason: they are aware that the Mainlanders hardly ever think of them. Aus-tralians do not care much about anybody or anything that is not constantly right in front of their noses: and Tasmania is too small and too remote to catch their eye often enough.

Tasmanians have to draw attention to their own fame, as no

one else is likely to do it for them. 'Our regatta is the greatest acquatic event in the Southern Hemisphere.' It is true that the Sydney-Hobart yacht race taking place every Christmas is the greatest yachting event on the Continent (I do not think I have to remind my readers in great detail that in Australia everything is the other way round: the further south one travels, the colder it becomes as one gets nearer to the Antarctic regions of the South Pole. Tasmania, as a result, is the coldest state in Australia. Being in the Southern Hemisphere, Australians usually celebrate Christmas in the middle of a heatwave and on the beaches – but with fir-trees and Father Christmases in long robes and with long beards; July and August are the coldest months, etc). Tasmanians are also proud of the devestating forest fire that broke out in that hot dry month, February 1967. The fire was terrible and Hobart itself was in grave danger of being devoured by it. But the whole world was watching Tasmania and it was her finest hour. It took a forest fire of such gigantic dimensions to push Hobart onto the front page of the world's newspapers. The people of Hobart point out to you the burnt out patches in the nearby forests; they boast about the damage and exaggerate the death-roll. 'Our own brewery was burnt down, you know,' a young man told me as proudly as if he himself had set fire to it.

The rhythm of life is slower and more dignified in Tasmania than on the Mainland and they are rightly proud of that, too. Their approach to many problems is more easy-going and light-hearted, less intense and less worried than that of the Mainlanders. They despise hurry and fail to see any point in it. When they talk of the Mainland, phrases like 'mad rush', 'rat-race' and 'hectic commuters – or whatever you call them' recur. But when it comes to football, all this reserve and detachment are thrown to the wind. They are even more fanatical about the game than Victorians and it is claimed that more people play it *per capita* in Tasmania than anywhere else in Australia. And – as we are talking of Australian football – that means than anywhere in the world; certainly than anywhere in the Southern Hemisphere.

Throughout the centuries millions of Tasmanians were born,

lived and died without leaving the island. Today travelling has become much easier. 'Travelling' still most often means flying to Sydney, Melbourne or Adelaide but a growing number of young Tasmanians go abroad, mostly to London.

Tasmania is tiny by Australian standards, about 26,000 square miles, roughly the size of Scotland and rather less than a third of the area of Victoria, by far the smallest of the mainland states. Its population is 370,000 (a little more than one tenth of that of Scotland, not an overpopulated country either). More than half of the people live in Hobart, the capital (125,000 inhabitants) and Launceston, Tasmania's second city in the north of the island, with more than 60,000 people. Tasmania is a colourful and beautiful land, and Hobart, with its splendid harbour and impressive site at the foot of Mount Wellington, is a charming and endearing city – having more of the colonial style than most other Australian cities. The graceful Tasman Bridge across the River Derwent even reminds one of Sydney Harbour Bridge. It was finished in 1963, replacing a less efficient, less beautiful but more romantic floating bridge.

Tasmania's varied landscape and great natural beauty brings in hosts of tourists, about 200,000 of those despised Mainlanders every year. Tasmania at first resented this invasion but then woke up – as she is slowly waking up in all respects – and the newly formed Tourist Association performs a useful job very well. But there are no international luxury hotels in Tasmania, no fancy cuisine, no night-clubs, no strip-tease shows and no casino. The City Fathers – and the elders of the state – have decreed that those who come to Tasmania are to enjoy the country's natural beauty and that's that. Those who come certainly do enjoy it as there is plenty of natural beauty to enjoy; but some people, having enjoyed the beauty of nature during the day, like to enjoy the beauty of a girl's thighs or a bit of roulette at night. These people, of course, stay away; 'Let them,' murmur the City Fathers of Hobart in unison. For those who come, Tasmania has one decided advantage over all other Australian cities: the Australian traveller feels abroad, yet he has the reassuring sensation of being able to speak the language.

Tasmania has other industries besides tourism and apples (apples being Tasmania's best known produce in Britain). There is a growing manufacturing industry of all sorts and a lot of mining. Tasmania is the only state of Australia which is rich in water and, as a result, also in hydro-electric power. This is responsible for the great post-war upsurge of industrial development; indeed, Tasmania's hydro-electric power potential is only a little less than that of the entire Mainland. The island is

also remarkable for its fauna, its peculiar mammals constituting its main claim to fame. As Australia was in her day separated off from the world land-mass, so was Tasmania separated from Australia a hundred million years later – give or take a few dozen million years, what does it matter? – thus preserving a few animals which are now extinct everywhere else, including the Mainland. The *Pocket Year Book of Tasmania* (1966) remarks: 'Australia may be regarded ... as a vast sanctuary in which primitive mammals were preserved from the destructive inroads of higher forms, and Tasmania, through its conversion into an island, became in fact a sanctuary within a sanctuary.' Apart from a dozen kinds of native rats and bats, there are two indigenous mammalian groups: the Monotremes, revealing something about our reptilian, egg-laying ancestors (the platypus and the spiny anteater are the two living representatives of this group), and the inevitable marsupials, of which Tasmania has twenty different kinds (including the kangaroos and wallabies); about ten of these are peculiar to Tasmania, to the pleasure of the Tasmanian zoologists and, alas, to the even greater pleasure of the Tasmanian fur-industry.

'Tasmania is the Sicily of Australia,' a Mainlander living in Hobart and hating it intensely, told me. 'Not only because it is a large island at the foot of the country. The underworld is similar, too; and Tasmanians are as vindictive as Sicilians. No slight, injury or injustice – real or imaginary – is ever forgotten, let alone forgiven.'

No one else mentioned to me the existence of a Tasmanian Mafia and I am more than doubtful about it. But many people spoke similarly about Tasmanian vindictiveness which seems to be almost tribal and Arabian in its longevity and ferocity.

Tasmania – a small island *beyond* a faraway continent – is coming nearer to the rest of humanity, to its own great sorrow. It will be a sad day for Tasmania when the first hectic commuter – 'or whatever you call them' – appears with his rimless spectacles and briefcase, but the day cannot be long delayed. All the same, this beautiful and, at the moment, leisurely island is neither so remote nor so small as a remark made by a visiting multi-millionaire American business-man implied. He was told all about Tasmanian history, was given all the statistics about tourism, industry, mining and hydro-electric plants – then he interrupted impatiently: 'That's all very well. What I want to know is – who *owns* the place.'

Adelaide

There is a story beloved by Australian after-dinner speakers about the first question a visitor is bound to be asked in various Australian cities. In Melbourne they will ask him which club he belongs to; in Sydney, how much money he makes, and so on; the points vary according to where the joke is being told. But they will not differ on one point: in Adelaide, all agree, the first question you are asked is: which church do you go to? But that after-dinner speech is a little out-of-date today.

Adelaide – no longer just a city of churches – is a charming place. With its well-planned boulevards and alleys, gardens and large parks it reminds one of Canberra. The widest of these thoroughfares are called, for some reason, terraces; and the North Terrace, with Government House, the war memorial, the public library, some big hotels and other impressive, not ultra-modern business-houses, is the pride of the city. Adelaide is more colonial in style than Canberra because it is older. But by European standards it is a very young city, barely a teenager. The so-called Colonization Act, establishing the Province of South Australia, was passed by the British Parliament in 1834 and Adelaide, its capital, was incorporated in 1840.

There was no convict settlement in these parts: the first settlers were Germans from Silesia. For a long time Adelaide was ruled by a haughty Establishment – a narrow-minded, ultra-conservative oligarchy consisting basically of a few families and congregating in the Adelaide Club. Their influence has not disappeared yet but it has been weakened and goes on weakening. This ruling class is puritanic and religious, not so much for the sake of God Almighty as for its own sake: its leaders know that religion is the most powerful force for conservatism and they also know that all change helps to dig their own graves as a class. These people ruled Adelaide unchallenged for a long time. Then, for a period, all Australian state governments gained a bad reputation for corruption and intrigue and the reputation of South Australia ranked among the worst. But that period has also passed. Today, in the third period, more and more industrialists are moving into South

Australia – into Adelaide or Elizabeth or near these cities – and while the influence of the industrialist is not unmitigated bliss, he brings with him an air of the twentieth century, a breath of energy and ambition. The industrialists' clash with the plutocracy is as inevitable as their ultimate victory over the declining class. The old oligarchy clings to the past; the new oligarchy thrives on change and on keeping up-to-date. Yet, the duel has undertones of subtlety: the industrialists are determined not only to conquer the old, prestigious class but also to undermine

145

it from within, by becoming part of it. They want to lick them and join them at one and the same time. They infiltrate the Adelaide Club, strike up friendships with the old families, marry their daughters and buy land, try their hands at shooting and between manufacturing more plastic mugs and assembling more automobiles, they play the part of the South Australian version of the landed gentry and the part-time grazier.

Adelaide is an extremely agreeable place to live in. It has an atmosphere of kindliness and relaxation, people are affluent and smiling, helpful and polite. It is a pleasant experience to walk about the wide terraces or listen to the birds in the parks. Adelaide is also becoming the Edinburgh of Australia: it has a biennial Arts Festival, with a large number of notable musicians, orchestras, conductors and other artists taking part. It is a conservative occasion, not much new ground is broken here but it is on an increasingly high level and does a great amount of good to the arts as well as to Adelaide.

The capital may be prosperous but South Australia itself is not a very prosperous state because it is dry – the driest of all the states in a notoriously dry continent – and it is also very sparsely populated. In fact, more than half of it is practically uninhabited. South Australia is as big as Western Europe but the entire state has no more inhabitants than Birmingham – just over a million. And 600,000 of them live in Adelaide.

The most famous of South Australia's industries is vine-growing in the Barossa Valley. The valley starts about thirty miles north-east of Adelaide, is eighteen miles long and five miles wide and it produces from one third to one half of all the country's wines and about eighty per cent of its brandy. It is still a very German-looking district, with old German cottages and a pretty little Lutheran church in each small village. Barossa Valley got its name from a Spanish wine-growing district and the wines, too, have European names – burgundy and claret, port and muscat. I could not discover one Australian name in the lot but whatever their names, they are excellent wines, better than anything I have tasted outside Europe and better than many I have tasted inside Europe. And certainly better than the wines of California where I once saw an advertisement *'Californian Burgundy – Beware of French Imitations'*. Once again it was the migrants who were responsible for the increasing prosperity of the wine industry. It was they who taught Australians to drink wine with their meals; before the Great Migration Australians thought that to drink anything other than beer was both illegal and sacrilegious.

If South Australia has plenty of wine, it certainly has not enough water. It is the Murray River that helps out: a fifty mile pipeline leads from the river to Adelaide and nearly 230 miles of pipeline leads from the Murray at Morgan to the steelworks at Whyalla. The length of this pipeline is extremely important. South Australia needs to boast of some achievement – don't we all? – and it can claim altogether four national or international records.

First, the Morgan-Whyalla pipeline is the longest in the world, or in the Southern Hemisphere, or in all the English-speaking countries. In any case, it is the longest somewhere. Second, the River Murray with its four hundred miles is the longest river of Australia. Third, South Australia is the only Australian state which has a common frontier with all the other mainland states as well as the Northern Territory (some people remark that this simply follows from her geographical position and is not a real achievement – but this is jealous carping). The fourth record was a little more difficult to find. But it has been found. Westward from Adelaide, across the Nullarbor Plain, we find the *world's longest stretch of straight railway-track* It's not a very good railway; not very comfortable; not very punctual. But, Gee, isn't that track long! And straight!

Perth

Western Australia wears a disguise. She is regarded as a huge, isolated state; beautiful and distant and famous for her wild flowers and eternal sunshine; sleepy, easygoing, poor and of little consequence. Attitudes and states of mind change more slowly than reality. Western Australia laughs up her sleeve and it is the rest of the country which is half asleep now; it is the rest of the country which – as far as Western Australia is concerned – has to wake up and reassess its values.

Some of the truth of yesterday, of course, remains the truth of today. Western Australia is just as huge as it used to be. Our European imagination boggles at its vastness. I mentioned in the last chapter that South Australia was huge and sparsely populated. That is true; yet, compared with Western Australia South Australia is a Belgium: tiny and thickly populated.

Western Australia is three times as large but has only eighty per cent of South Australia's population. This single state of Australia is ten times as large as the United Kingdom (complete with Northern Ireland) but has only one tenth of the population of London (not even Greater London; just London). For those few people who prefer plain figures to staggering comparisons: Western Australia is nearly one million square miles in area and she has 800,000 inhabitants, of whom more than half – 450,000 – live in Perth, the capital. This means a density of about one person to the square mile. If the families of Western Australia were evenly distributed, each family could have five square miles to itself. Western Australia is the largest state of the Commonwealth, occupying 32.8 per cent of its territory but having only 7.1 per cent of its population. It has always been rich in sheep, wheat and timber; and also in gold. The state produces almost eighty per cent of Australia's gold.

Western Australia then is as large as ever, and although not quite so isolated as it used to be, it is still pretty isolated. A city can feel just as lonely as a human being and Perth is the loneliest city in the whole wide world. It is as far from Sydney as Chicago is from Los Angeles. The nearest and most easily accessible city is Adelaide which is nearly as far from Perth as London is from Istanbul. And the two cities are divided from each other by vast, uninhabitable and unexplored desert and scrubland. To its west is the infinite Indian Ocean.

There it is then, lonely Perth, beautiful yet unwanted, most desirable yet undesired. This loneliness has evoked in the hearts of the people of Perth the usual human response: 'If you don't want me, I don't want you either; if you are happy without me, I'm even happier without you.' When the Federation was formed, Western Australia sulked a little and meant to stay outside. She still mistrusts the East and the East starts on her border; it certainly includes South Australia which, in turn, also mistrusts the East. In spite of all this, Western Australia in this jet age could not help getting a little nearer to other parts than she used to be. Not so long ago it took a week's boat journey to get to Perth from Sydney; my ANA plane took me there in under four hours. Perth used to be lonely; soon it will remember the days nostalgically when it *could* be lonely and was left alone.

Perth is very beautiful[1] with its fine Narrow Bridge across the delta of the Swan River, and with its lovely and well-kept parks full of wild flowers – 7,000-odd species of them, reputedly the loveliest wild flowers in the world. These famous flowers, now legally protected from indiscriminate picking, bring thousands of visitors in spring-time. The most famous of all the flowers is the Kangaroo Paw, Western Australia's floral emblem. The Kangaroo Paw is exclusive to south Western Australia, has very curiously shaped flowers and coloured vestiture of plume-like, interlocked hairs. It exists in seven varieties and in a countless variety of colours: red and yellow, yellow and green, green and purple, red and green and sooty black.

The visitor from the East admires these wild flowers, takes notes of the parks and the view, and also of the sunshine (eight hours average per day, throughout the year); he observes the old-fashioned house sandwiched between huge, ultra-modern office buildings, and he nods. Yes, Western Australia is a mixture of old and new, ancient and modern; she is half asleep, so all is well.

This observation is not entirely groundless.

A friend of mine, a distinguished Hungarian poet, was imprisoned by the Communists in the early fifties; in the concentration camp he happened to get hold of a Western Australian stamp. This caught his imagination and, in his misery, he wrote a beautiful poem about Western Australia, its discovery, and the long trek from the East; in his imagination he saw the brave Eastern frontiersmen struggling westward. But all this is simply an imaginary parallel with the conquest of the American Wild West. There was no westward trek in Australia. The colonization of the East began at the end of the eighteenth century and went on for a long time, without anybody bothering about the West. On May 2, 1829 Captain

---

[1] The reader may wonder if I see all Australian state capitals as beautiful. I do not. First of all, I am speaking of their situation, not of their architectural beauty. Then, I call Sydney, Hobart and Perth beautiful; Melbourne and Adelaide are pleasant and even impressive; Brisbane is rather indifferent.

Charles Fremantle – who gave his name to the port, twelve miles from Perth – arrived at the mouth of the Swan River, hoisted the British flag and, in the name of His Majesty King George IV, took possession of 'all that part of New Holland which is not included within the Territory of New South Wales.' The colonies in the east and in the west grew up independently of each other and it was long before regular communication was established between them. As a result Western Australia is neither Western nor Australia. At least some of her people still wonder whether the East regards them as proper Australians, with all the rights of a proper Aussie. But it is not 'western' either, in the European and American sense: it is southern and even slightly oriental. The mentality of Western Australia reminds one of southern Spain: it has the equanimity of the *'mucha calma'* and the *'mañana, mañana'* spirit; people are relaxed and easy-going; time does not matter much. If you have an appointment but find something better to do, well, tomorrow will be another day. And what if you miss that appointment altogether?

Much of this spirit still survives. This misleads the Eastern visitor who often fails to notice that Western Australia woke up in secret. It has become a great industrial state and is developing faster than most other parts of the land. Gold has always been there and the early fortunes were made from gold, not always legally. Not all the gold found its way into the mint and quite a lot goes astray even today. Detectives are active but what can they do in a country of this size where one can travel hundreds of miles without meeting a living soul? I was told that it is possible to strike gold, open a mine and operate it for years without being discovered. Many families, reputable today, became rich this way; just as many reputable European and American families became rich in much more dishonest ways.

But gold is the old story. 1960 ushered in an industrial revolution of tremendous importance. 100,000 acres of new land, mostly in the north, have been opened up; large amounts of new minerals and metals have been found and are being developed: iron ore has lately stolen the limelight (with Japanese steel-companies exploring it) but there are many other precious finds; paper mills are being built; petroleum and lubricating oil refineries are being opened; in 1963 a vast aluminium refinery started production at Kwinana – already an important industrial centre – to process bauxite from the Darling Ranges, near Perth; in the same year, a large titanium oxide treatment plant was opened at Bunbury (echoes of Oscar Wilde?) and cement production too is starting up in earnest. And so on and so on. If I were a young man with a future (instead of being a terribly middle-aged man without much of a past) or a speculator, I would move to Western Australia. If the whole of Australia is the land of a fast-approaching future – a future which is already knocking at the door – Western Australia has an even brighter future within that future. The Eastern visitor cannot help noticing that estate prices in Perth are already almost as high as they are in Sydney or Melbourne. Other prices are still lower and so are wages. But not for long. Western Australia's sleepiness and contempt for time is just a tradition, the preservation of a civilized attitude; the breathless rush, the permanent hurry is the habit of the neo-barbarians. Otherwise Western Australia is wide awake – and that is the disguise I mentioned earlier. Under this mask of easygoing Mediterranean carelessness, a new industrial state is booming. Western Australia does not mind if she *looks* poor. People pay low taxes because this is a claimant state, which means that she is entitled to help from the Commonwealth. She is, surely, the richest beggar in the world. She is getting richer and richer every day, but her people still refuse to hurry and all those wild flowers bloom in the spring, tra-la-la.

Attitudes die hard on both side, not only in the East. A new friend told me in Perth:

'What do you mean by saying that we were not a convict settlement? We are a convict-settlement even today. Easterners dump their rejects on us. The days of colonization are not over yet. The rest of Australia is becoming a colony of America and Japan. Why, they say that even the Church of England is being replaced by the Church of America. But *we* are not in danger, we won't become a colony of America and Japan. We are going to remain a colony of the rest of Australia.'

Alice

Alice Springs is the second biggest town in the Northern Territory; and the Northern Territory covers more than a million square miles. It is two and a half times as large as France and six times the size of Britain; it covers one sixth of Australia. The distance between its northern and southern extremities is as great as the distance between London and Stockholm. Darwin, on the tropical northern edge of Australia, is about as near to the main cities of South East Asia as it is to Melbourne.

So it is somewhat surprising to learn that the second city of this vast expanse is in fact a village of 6,000 people.[1] The biggest town, Darwin, has 16,881 inhabitants, about 2,000 less than Chippenham, Wiltshire. But, after all, the size of a town is not everything. Both Darwin and Alice Springs (commonly and affectionately referred to as Alice) captured my heart, if for different reasons. The capital used to be called Palmerston and changed its name to Darwin. It is not usual for a town to discard the name of a politician for the name of a scientist.

Alice Springs, on the other hand, is the dream of politicians, and particularly the dream of Postmaster Generals; or Postmasters General, if you insist. It is not often that these hardworking but unromantic gentlemen are immortalized. It was as late as in 1871 that a man named William Whitefield Mills, a surveyor employed by the Post Office, discovered a large waterhole (a billabong, I daresay) at the foot of a rocky hill,

[1] As usual, six official publications give five different figures. If I relied on a majority verdict, I would report that Alice Springs has only just over 5,000 people. But the official handbook, *Australia,* puts the figure at 6,076.

practically at the geometrical centre of the continent of Australia and named it Alice Springs, after Lady Todd, the wife of his boss, Sir Charles Todd, the Postmaster General. And as if this were not enough, he named the near-by river Todd. No PMG can expect more from any of his surveyors. I hope Mr Mills got his promotion.

Alice – small though it may be – is a lovable town, with a sharp profile and marked personality, so rare among Australian towns. The place has a charm and an atmosphere quite of its own. Alice Springs was the second place in Australia where I felt: this is an indigenous growth, a true Australian town, belonging to Australia alone which could not be anywhere else. (The second place, you notice: nothing will induce me to say whether Sydney or Melbourne was the first.) Alice Springs is Alice Springs, right at the heart of Australia, and it could not be shifted either to Co. Durham or to Kansas, USA and remain the same – as is the case with many other Australian localities. The town itself is not beautiful or full of memorable buildings; it has more personality than beauty although its neighbourhood is extremely beautiful. In Alice it is the atmosphere of the place that catches you.

'I was born and brought up in Adelaide,' a new acquaintance told me, 'and I was twenty-six when I was sent to Alice, first time in my life, on a job. I saw Alice and fell in love with it: I knew that this was the place I wanted to live. I came here and have stayed here ever since. There is an informality and lack of pomposity here which are slowly dying out everywhere else. People drop in on one another without ringing up first – well few people have telephones anyway – for a chat or a drink together. Perhaps it turns into a party, perhaps an argument, perhaps nothing at all. But there is always tomorrow. Friends are friends here and the phrase, "a good friend of mine" retains its meaning here. We have only one radio station and if someone succeeds in getting Brisbane, he is as happy as a European radio-amateur is when he gets the Cocos Islands. We have no TV. Perhaps television will come to Alice one day. That will be the day I leave.'

He had become acclimatized to the town more than he

realized. We crossed the river and I remarked that there was no water in it.

'There isn't,' he agreed. 'Most of the time it's dry. But sometimes it is not. Occasionally it floods Alice and cuts the city into two.'

'How do you communicate then?' I asked.

'We don't. Because we can't. It just isn't possible. One half of the town is on one side, the other half on the other side. There is no way of crossing over.'

'But that must be terribly inconvenient and cause an awful lot of trouble.'

'Why should it?' he asked me in genuine surprise. 'It only lasts for a fortnight or so. Perhaps even less.'

*   *   *

The Northern Territory hopes to become a state one day but it is not a state yet. Just a Territory. Its administration is the

responsibility of the Federal Government and it is governed by a Legislative Council, presided over by the Administrator. The Governor-General of Australia appoints (on the recommendation of the Administrator) six official and three unofficial members to the Council, and there are also eight elected members. The official members may be removed at the Governor's pleasure, and appointed members outnumber elected ones at any time. So this Legislative Council is not a rebellious body and has little chance (or desire) to become one. The Territory has 50,000 inhabitants, of whom 20,000 are full-blooded Aborigines. (Aborigines are conspicuous in Alice: they are numerous and ubiquitous, hanging around at street corners, going about their business, ambling around – some of them jumping in and out of taxis. But most of them are not to be seen: they live in reserves and are being looked after with care. A few hundred of them are still nomads. About four hundred are in regular, reasonably good employment and twenty are being trained as government forestry officers. I have written about Aborigines elsewhere in this book.)

The density of population in the Northern Territory is one person per ten square miles. Not exactly a second China.

It was in 1872 that a telegraph line, traversing Australia from south to north, was completed. It consisted of one single piece of wire and it was Australia's (and Alice's) sole connection with the outside world.

The North has a tough story to tell. Several attempts at its settlement failed and had to be abandoned. Its overland exploration began in 1845 when Ludwig Leichhardt travelled from Brisbane to Port Essington. It was in 1861 that Burke and Wills traversed the Continent – a famous and often described epic. Alice Springs itself was, not so long ago, at a tremendous distance from civilization. Not only old, even middle-aged people will remember the days when it took six weeks for camel caravans to get to Alice from Adelaide. Then in 1928 the railways came and the time of travel was cut to a week. I flew up in two hours.

The war ushered in a new period. Darwin was first bombed by the Japanese in February, 1942, and the attacks went on for a while. It was the war in general and the attacks on Darwin in particular that speeded up road-building and the Stuart Highway – nearly a thousand miles long – was built between Alice Springs and Darwin, and the Barkly Highway to Queensland was completed soon afterwards. The Northern Territory is developing slowly and I personally hope it will soon reach the august status of statehood. But it is not yet one of the famous centres of civilization. When the railway was finished in 1928, the total population of this Central Australian region was estimated at four hundred people. And even today an official publication lists the three main towns – I repeat: main towns after Darwin and Alice – as follows: Tennant Creek, population 972; Katherine, population 770; Batchelor, population 470.

* * *

Alice Springs has two claims to international fame. It figured in the title of Neville Shute's best-selling novel, *A Town like Alice* (the title of the film, too) and secondly – perhaps mostly – because it is the headquarters of the Flying Doctor Service which has captured the imagination of people all over the world. The Service was the idea, in the twenties, of the Rev. Dr John Flynn of the Australian Inland Mission. Today the Flynn Memorial Church is one of the attractive sights of Alice Springs.

Probably every hospital in the Scottish Highlands has more patients and more doctors than the Royal Flying Doctors Service of Australia. But no medical establishment of the world has a larger territory to look after: a quarter of a million square miles, three times the territory of Britain. In the country of which Alice is the centre, there are cattle stations, mining centres, geological research posts, bush parties – all of them isolated. A farm covering a thousand square miles worked by eight or ten people is no rarity. The largest concentration of people is a hundred and thirty, on a cattle-station covering five thousand square miles. A doctor may fly five hundred miles (i.e. a thousand miles round trip) to attend a patient.

I visited the Headquarters of the Flying Doctors, a small and unpretentious house in Alice Springs. Its nerve centre is the radio-room. Every morning one of the doctors has a session and any patient who cares to talk to him can ring him up on the radio-telephone. This practice reminds one of the practice of doctors in the United States. It is the almost universal habit there for a doctor to have an hour on the phone every morning. During this hour he picks up the phone and any patient who has a query, a complaint, a remark or a report to make, can pour out his heart. The system here is the same, but the distances and, consequently, the importance of these consultations, are very different. In Alice they are very informal and human and it is first of all the soothing voice of the doctor which brings comfort to the patient or to his worried mother. 'Good morning doctor,' you hear dozens of times every morning and the soothing voice replies:

'What about those tablets now? . . . They don't seem to be too effective, do they? Well, we'll try this-or-that instead. I'll send it up to you today. If it is unobtainable, I'll send the next best thing.'

'Yes, yes, penicillin can be given intra-muscularly. Two shots to be given straight away. After tea another half million units. From then on quarter of a million units per day. If the child is not better by tomorrow morning, call me again.'

The doctor is kind and understanding but there is no sob-stuff and no sentimentality. That would be very un-medical and un-Australian. He is always most informal.

'And don't worry about those chickens either. The chickens will be on Monday's plane.'

But the soothing voice is not always sufficient. There are four ways the service can help:

(1) The doctor – as we have seen – questions the patient and gives him instructions. People have medical kits, well equipped. The kits – there are two hundred fixed stations and a hundred mobile units – are absolutely the same everywhere, so it is easy for the doctor to explain where the patient can find the required drug. Each patient has a card and every piece of advice and instruction given is recorded on it.

(2) If there is a fracture or minor injury, or the ailment seems to be slight, or if it is a woman in labour, a nurse (who is also a midwife) flies out. The stations may be remote from Alice but all are accessible by plane. There are nearly two hundred airports or landing strips in the Territory.

(3) If the case is more serious, a doctor flies out.

(4) In some cases the pilot flies out alone and brings the patient in.

A report is made of each flight. Reports go something like this:

'Aboriginal girl, named Sarah, about twenty, suffering from broken arm. Sister Ellis attended the flight.'

'Aboriginal boy, aged six, kicked by bullock, severe pain in stomach. Patient is losing weight alarmingly. Sister Howell attended the flight.'

'Twenty-six-years-old employee of the Meteorological Service admitted to Oodnadatta Hostel with serious eye injury. Splashed on chest and face with molten lead. Injuries include large blob of lead adhering to corner of left eye. Dr Pitts attended the flight.'

They also make out monthly reports: March, 1967. White: 91, Black 289. Miles flown: 5,509.

About a hundred thousand miles are flown every year. The service has two planes, a Beechcraft and a Cessna; their average speed is 150 m.p.h. In the twelve month period mentioned they carried '1,372 white and 4,669 black.' They are not even added up, to make a joint total of persons. They are not treated for skin diseases, where this black or white business might be of some importance. One would expect the kidneys, gall-bladders and diaphragms of people to be the same for doctors – and of the same colour, too. This colour discrimination in the reports does the Flying Doctors a disservice. When it comes to ordinary human need, there is no discrimination whatsoever; the Aboriginal girl 'named Sarah, about twenty' is treated as readily and kindly as the white geologist.

From the headquarters of the Flying Doctors they also maintain – using their excellent radio – a school service. This is how solitary children – or children in tiny groups – at those isolated stations receive their education.

'Good morning, David. Thank you for the little dog. We call him Whisky. Do you think Whisky is a good name?'

'Now, you draw a banana. And now another. That makes two bananas. Now you add five more bananas. That's right: five more. What is the result? Well done, Dennis, you do draw bananas well.'

When I was about to leave the headquarters of the Flying Doctors, a middle-aged farmer came in and we started talking. He told me he lived at one of the isolated stations, 382 miles from Alice, and had four children. I asked him if he ever felt that it was dangerous for the children to live so far away from medical help? What would happen in a serious emergency?

'Dangerous? I assure you this is a better service than we used to get in town. You ring up and speak to the doctor himself without any fuss. You can get into hospital more quickly than from most Australian suburbs. Last time I rang the doctor at 8.30 – my younger daughter was very sick – and at 11.30 the doctor was by her bedside. In the suburb where we had lived before, the doctor would not have turned up before 4.30 in the afternoon. And those town doctors rush in, give a quick glance at the patient, write something on a piece of paper and they are gone. If a doctor flies 382 miles to see you, he will pay some attention to you. If for no other reason than that he doesn't want to come back. If you are a fellow who needs doctors often and quickly, I'll give you this advice: leave that famous London of yours and move to a cattle-station, 400 miles from Alice Springs.'

* * *

Tourism has become a major industry of Alice Springs. Some people are attracted by the flora and the fauna of the region. There is an iguana-type lizard there, called the horned dragon, or *maloch horridus*. It grows to seven inches in length and its appearance is really fearsome; but it is a gentle and harmless creature, often kept as a pet. On the list of local birds I found one called the Major Mitchell Cockatoo. I was dying to see a Major Mitchell Cockatoo but failed. Knowing my luck, I fear

I shall never see one. Most of the tourists, however, come to see other beauties of nature, first of all Ayers Rock – the largest single rock in the world whose reddish mass can be observed from a plane twelve miles away. There are many gorges – a large number of beautiful and extraordinary formations – and numerous gaps. Mostly gaps. If you love and appreciate gaps, Alice Springs is the place for you.

But if you love and appreciate good coffee, you must choose some other place. I was offered a cup of coffee by a charming old lady and she asked:

'Do you take salt in it?'

To my amazement, she put it in hers. I told her that personally I did not take salt.

'I see, you take it with lemon,' she said brightly and put a slice of lemon, attached to the end of a toothpick, in my coffee.

*   *   *

Most of the Northern Territory lies in the tropics. Its climate is not only tropical but also monsoonal. Alice – not in the tropics – has marked extremes of temperature. I expected boiling heat there but came late in the year (May – corresponding to our November) and I froze on the first day. It is not unusual in Alice Springs to have 100° Fahrenheit and the maximum temperature recorded is 115°. When the thermometer starts falling, it does not know where to stop: 19° Fahrenheit has been known. A chance acquaintance said goodbye to me in the bar of my hotel.

'I'm off to warmer climates,' he informed me.

'Going to Queensland?' I asked.

'Oh no. To London.'

Paradise

The airport at the near-by Queensland town still looks quite normal. Then you drive along the 'Gold Coast', towards Surfers Paradise (thus named – it was explained to me at some length – because it is a paradise for surfers) and the landscape changes. For miles and miles on end, every single house offers you holiday flats to let; or is a motel; or a garage. All the houses are small, styleless and graceless, they seem to have been thrown together just to last out the holiday season. There are villas, too and you study their names: Sarana, Kingalonga, Shalimar; Ocean Front; Neptune and Ibiscus; Koala Bear. Suddenly you reach the Beefburger Belt, where Beefburgers are cooked and offered for sale in every house. A flood of beefburgers; an ocean of beefburgers. Only a few cheeseburgers here and there break the monotony. I breathed with relief and delight when I saw a sign: FISHO.

Some of the restaurant advertisements are on the cosy side: FILL UP HERE, they invite you.

'Restaurant Open', 'Flat Vacant'. Then, you reach the area of larger and better-built houses; there are even a few sky-scrapers. You have arrived in Surfers Paradise itself. By this time you have acclimatized. I was haunted by two main problems. I tried to figure out: how many beefburgers would fill up the sky-scraper. I also wondered who was the man – an American, that's clear – who first decided that the word Hamburger has nothing to do with the city of Hamburg but consisted of two words: ham and burger. This is the man who is responsible for cheeseburgers, steakburgers, nutburgers and beefburgers. If he died without ever noticing that hamburgers do not contain ham, let him rest in peace; if he is still alive, he should be sent into eternal exile to Beefburg. Or to Surfers Paradise.

This place is a mixture of Southend, Hawaii, Coney Island and hell. I walked into a bookshop to look around. It was the first bookshop I've ever been in where I could not spot a book – not just a book I liked: any book at all. There were greeting cards, picture postcards, funny drawings, mugs, plates, souvenirs, toys and comics: but not one single book. I walked back to the street – with somewhat uncertain steps: orders and commands shrieked at me from all directions. Rent a Car! Rent a Paddle Boat! See *Two* Floor-Shows! Have an International Coffee! (Even in my dazed state of mind this intrigued me so I went in to see what an 'international coffee' might mean. It meant that you could get German, Dutch, Swiss or Turkish Coffee.) Rent a Second Car! Buy a Flat for Investment! Take Home a Hot Dog!

I am easily persuaded and I do what I am told. I bought a few flats for investment and tried to take a hot dog home. Anything, just to get home. But it was not to be. On my way home I was instructed: 'Take Part in a Hawaiian Feast'.

I reached my hotel, eventually. It was the best and most expensive hotel in the place. If I remember rightly I paid one million dollars for a night. I had been after paradoxes and peculiarities – I pondered ruefully – and now I had got all the paradoxes and contradictions one could dream of. I had enjoyed hot summer weather in Sydney although it was late autumn and everybody had warned me that it would be cold and rainy. I met even hotter weather in antarctic Tasmania ('the hottest autumn for sixty-eight years!'). I had found Kings Cross, the gayest and noisiest spot on the continent, deserted and dull. Now I had reached Surfers Paradise in Queensland, the state which is called 'the gateway to the tropics' (a bit of a misnomer as the greater part of the state is actually in the tropics) and I found the place chilly, windy and unpleasant. I sat down by the hotel swimming pool. It was lit up with red, green and purple bulbs under the water and every single bulb spelt out the message of the place, its *genius loci:* life is a perpetual jamboree and a bookshop doesn't really need any books. I started playing a game I invented – find the lady with the largest behind, in tight, pink slacks. But at the semi-final stage I fell asleep, with a beefburger in each of my pockets, and had a nightmare: I dreamt that I was seeing Two Floor Shows and was having a Hawaiian Feast at the same time.

Off the coast of Queensland – in places a mere twenty miles away – is the Great Barrier Reef, one of the wonders of nature,

a wonderland of coral structures and magnificent, tropical fish, which is well worth a long extra journey to see.

I went on to Brisbane. I meant to sing an ode to Brisbane. Every visitor to Australia derides Brisbane and is nasty about it; calls it tropical, provincial, dusty, uninspiring, a city of managers and a poor satellite to Sydney and Melbourne. I was determined to be different, to love Brisbane. But Brisbane did not permit me to love it. The city – which contains forty per cent of Queensland's population, 650,000 people out of one

million and a half – has a reasonably attractive City Hall
(described as 'majestic' in these parts), some good shops and a
lot of people in shirtsleeves. Queenslanders have the reputation
of being chummy and friendly but I found even the Public
Relations Department cool and stand-offish. It was really my
own fault: elsewhere in Australia I had been spoilt, in fact
overwhelmed with attention, so here I left too much to chance,
simply rang up the Public Relations Department, introduced
myself and mentioned the name of the Chief Public Relations
Officer of the Commonwealth Government who had sent me to
them. The Brisbane gentleman was most courteous and said he
would send me some literature. 'I don't think I can do more for
you', he told me. Perhaps he couldn't. The literature arrived
within ten minutes, sent by special messenger. It consisted of
two pamphlets which one could pick up at any travel agent's
counter plus a small picture-book. From the pamphlets I
learned that the Centenary Swimming Pool on Gregory
Terrace contained a children's wading pool. Further, I learnt
that 'at night, dinner-dances and floor shows are provided at
several hotels' and that 'steaks are a speciality at some dining
spots'. I pass this information on to my readers. If they want
more when in Brisbane, perhaps they should contact the
Information Officer directly. On my last day I saw 'tropical
fruit' on the breakfast menu, so I ordered it.

'What have you got?' I asked the waitress.

'Apples, pears, apricots.'

'But these are not very tropical.'

'No, not very.'

'But we are in the tropics. What happened to your papaya
and mango?'

She, with tight lips: 'We have apples, pears and apricots.'

Before leaving Brisbane I bought a nail-brush which fell to
pieces two days later. I also bought some deodorant for men
which caused a slight inflammation of the skin.

4 THREE STUDIES IN COLONIZATION

FRENCH: Tahiti

I felt certain that those twenty-five men flying with me in the same plane to Tahiti were members of a large dancing group. They were young and slim; had black hair and flashing eyes; their manners were a mixture of shyness and self-confidence, as is often the case with young artists. But no, they were not dancers, the stewardess informed me, they were French naval cadets. They were involved, in one way or another, in the hydrogen-bomb tests, to be carried out soon on one of the coral atolls of the South Pacific. I sighed deeply.

I sighed even more deeply when we got out of the plane, around midnight, at Faaa airport. To be sure, there were five beautiful Tahitian girls, dressed in national costume, hanging garlands of flowers around the necks of tired and self-conscious American vice-presidents and their corpulent and peremptory wives. I declined with thanks, but little did I know the local habits. My name was called and a young lady from the Tourist Office approached me and, even before she greeted me, hung a *tiare heis* around my neck. Then the ground hostess of the airline came to shake hands with me but before doing so she adorned me with a garland. I had five garlands before I passed customs. The customs official gave me the sixth; and the woman taxi-driver who was to drive me to the hotel Taaone, the seventh. Before I got into her taxi, my eye caught a huge board informing us in several languages: TIPPING IS NOT CUSTOMARY IN TAHITI. 'God,' I sighed again, 'how hypocritical can you get.' But my deepest sigh of all was reserved for Papeete, the capital.

This famous city reminded me much more of my birthplace, Siklos, a sleepy and dusty little village in South Hungary, than of the romance of the South Pacific.

But soon enough I stopped sighing. 'You can't judge a place *thoroughly*,' I warned myself, 'after ten minutes. For that you need at least an hour.' That notice about tips was not hypocritical, for instance: not only do the Tahitians not expect a tip from you – they do not accept it either. It is true that refrigerator salesmen from Nebraska and half the vice-presidents of canned food companies from Kansas City looked just as odd with *tiare heis* around their necks as did an Anglo-Hungarian humorist from London, but there was nothing commercial in that welcome: the young ladies were employed by the Tourist Office and UTA the French airline, and their services, while cool and impersonal, were unselfish and free of charge. Papeete was, indeed, a hole and a village, (and even street-names like rue de General de Gaulle, rue Destremeau and rue Maréchal Foch fail to give it that truly French air so effortlessly worn by Noumea) but Tahiti, nevertheless, is still a lovable and romantic place, with an irresistible lure. (I have never felt the lure of places which, according to travel writers, I ought to have felt: the lure of the Mediterranean, the lure of Provence, the lure of the Greek islands, the lure of the West Indies. I liked them all and loved some of them dearly, but I was left unallured. Tahiti was the first place which really infected me: here, I felt, I could go on leading a lazy life indefinitely, chase women for the few remaining active years of my life and go to the dogs happily afterwards.) And those naval cadets. Yes, they were connected with atomic tests at Muruoa, 775 miles away, and not with the Romance of the South Pacific; nevertheless, while they are unlikely to cause any change in the balance of nuclear power, they have changed the sex-life and sex-habits of Tahiti.

* * *

Tahiti is in the depths of the South Pacific: about 6,000 miles away from Sydney and nearly as far from Hawaii. It is the most famous of the hundred and thirty islands of French

Polynesia – a territory larger than Europe (though most of it is water). Tahiti has 84,000 inhabitants, of whom 10,000 are Chinese, 8,000 French, 100 British and 400 other foreigners; fourteen of them are doctors and nine are dentists. This year they are expecting 16,000 tourists; last year they had 15,000, of whom 70 per cent were Americans and 18 per cent British (including Australians, New Zealanders and Canadians). 65,000 of the people are Tahitians, and half of them are women. They are all Gauguin types. You may see the *vahine* – the women of Tahiti – in *pareu*, a local dress compared with which the miniskirt is definitely much too long; the relationship of the miniskirt to the *pareu* is that of knitted Victorian bloomers to lace panties. Or you may see them on scooters or bicycles, plodding along in a traffic jam. But whether in *pareu* or on motor-scooters, they are Gauguin's women, Polynesians, some of the most beautiful women in the world whose only rivals are the Indonesian women of Bali. Our own *vahine*, French *vahine* or Italian *vahine* . . . well, it is the comparison of the *pareu* and the miniskirts all over again.

Sex and politics are curiously intermingled in Tahiti. The thoughts of all visiting male Europeans centre around women; the thoughts of Tahitians centre around Income Tax. (With the great difference, of course, that the *vahine* are desired and Income Tax is not.) In some colonial or ex-colonial territories oppression is dreaded; or malaria; or cholera; or the plague. In Tahiti oppression, malaria, cholera and the plague are all rolled into one; the idea of Income Tax. Tahitians pay no Income Tax, the country lives on indirect taxation and on excise duties and is, as a result, exorbitantly expensive. When de Gaulle ordered a plebiscite for all French possessions to decide whether they wanted (a) to become independent, (b) to become an integral part of France called Overseas Territories or (c) to keep their territorial status ('territory' is a new name for an old colony), the Tahitians decided to remain an ordinary territory, i.e. a colony. Proper French departments have their own representatives in the Parliament of Paris, that's true; but they also pay Income Tax. And the Tahitians reject all constitutional arrangements which include the paying of Income Tax.

They did not want to become independent, either. There are
rumblings, of course. Out of 23,000 voters, 9,000 voted against
maintaining the ties with France. Today out of Tahiti's
fourteen political parties (for 84,000 people!) three want
independence, the rest wish to stay with France. One party
violently resents the fact that after the loss of Algeria and her
deserts, France chose the atolls of the South Pacific as an atomic
test-ground. At the moment, Tahiti's Parliament has thirty
deputies who elect a government of five, while the Governor
himself is appointed by France. The Governor acts in dual
capacity: he is the head of the local government and also
represents French power. The assembly votes on the budget and
all local affairs. France looks after foreign affairs and defence
and also gives Tahiti a grant – free of charge, for no return
whatsoever – and finances education – which is compulsory and
free even at secondary level – roads, health services etc. The
French are the masters, and the masters are always slightly
detested, simply because they are the masters. But on the whole
this arrangement works pretty well.

France – haughty, Gaullist France which is supposed to
think in terms of continents and centuries only – chases
Tahiti with keen sexual fervour, in fact in the same manner as
visiting foreigners chase the *vahine*. France courts Tahiti in the
old-fashioned manner of the French Courts of Louis XIV and
XV, and Tahiti behaves as Mesdames Dubarry and Pompa-
dour did. France gets nothing out of Tahiti – even the phosphate
mines are closed now – indeed, the island costs her a great deal
of money. There is no illiteracy in Tahiti and most children,
even those on the outlying islands, speak French. There are good
roads; electricity and the telephone are everywhere, the social
and medical services are excellent and the standard of living is
high. A sick man may be flown three hundred miles to reach a
hospital where he will be looked after by a French doctor. And
for this tiny population there is a television service too. France
spoils Tahiti: partly because of prestige reasons but mostly for
love. Tahiti accepts France's adoration with a slight yawn and
with the bored air of a great and spoilt beauty.

As a French friend, living here, put it:

'Tahiti is listed as an underdeveloped territory. This is nonsense. Tahiti is spoilt, pampered and overdeveloped. Indeed, Tahiti and the United States are the only two over-developed territories in the world, struggling with all the horrid difficulties of overdevelopment. But France, it seems, wants it that way. Very well, as long as the phrase Income Tax is not uttered, France will be permitted to stay and pay homage.'

*　　*　　*

'Papeete may be ugly and smell of the supermarket and Tahiti isn't – that is the line many people try to sell you, but it is not entirely true. *Pisuppo* is ubiquitous. Tins of pea-soup were the first tins to arrive in Tahiti and since that moment *all* tins are called *pisuppo*. And *pisuppo* is as universally used in this island of romance, southern lure and French cuisine, as it is in that other overdeveloped land. Once upon a time Tahiti used to be Gauguin's island. Today it is Marlon Brando's island. A few years ago Brando made a film here – *Mutiny on the Bounty,* as this was the original venue – and while few Tahitians would refer to Gauguin, many mention Brando, with a gleam of pride in their eyes. Few would boast nowadays about Tahiti's only historical relic, the guillotine that cut off the head of Marie Antoinette, but many will point out relics and titbits left behind by the film-makers. Tourist pamphlets send you to the village of Anau, whose claim to fame is that it is the birthplace of a girl called Tarita, Marlon Brando's leading lady in *Mutiny.* Sometimes you recapture the lure of the South Pacific – as I did, entering a small bungalow with thatched roof or sitting under tall slender coconut trees, watching a Tahitian beauty on the right over the fence and admiring the lake-like calm of the distant Pacific; only to hear from the left, in broad Brooklynese: 'And what *is* the exchange rate, Alf?' Time, of course, marches on and it is no good repeating stubbornly that Papeete may change but Tahiti remains the same forever. *Tamaara* is the famous and traditional feast of the Tahitians, described in many romantic tales; but when I saw an advertise-ment in a travel agent's window referring glibly to a '*Tamaara-*

package', I became resigned to the fact that the whole world is going and Tahiti is going with it.

'Alas, you are quite right,' a new friend, an American expatriate told me, as we sat in his garden, under a palm tree and sipped Bourbon on the rocks. 'It was not so long ago – I remember it too well – that Tahiti was cut off from the world. Boats came in from Marseilles three or four times a year. That was a great and welcome event and, of course, the dream of all civil servants. Even after the war the situation was not too bad, although greatly changed. The planes of New Zealand airlines and UTA came in once a week, via Fiji. We besieged the post office for air mail but then the post closed down for two or three days – it had nothing to do. A few planes went to Bora-Bora too – the lovely tourist island nearby – and some Solent flying-boats brought a few more tourists from various islands. 1961 was the year of disaster: our isolation was broken, air-traffic began in earnest. Today we have about a dozen flights every week and their number is growing rapidly.'

He lit a cigarette.

'I'm longing to go to Mangareva. It's a little island, not far from here by South Pacific standards. It takes twenty-three days to get there by very small boat and once there, you have to wait thirty-two days to get a boat back. Wonderful.'

He looked into the smoke of his cigarette.

'We have remained an island in certain respects. When a ship calls, it is still an event and everyone comes out to see. But we have ceased to be an island in many other important ways and that's most disturbing. In the old days shops suddenly ran out of thread; or batteries; or pepper. Sudden shortages give you the feeling of living on an island. Today, all the shops are as well stocked as the supermarkets of Auckland, New Zealand.'

He stared at the distant sea for a moment.

'Give me back my shortages,' he said, 'and I'll be happy again.'

*   *   *

Race relations are good. The French never created the same

racial tensions as the British or, formerly, the Germans in Samoa or New Guinea. The Spaniards and the Portuguese stood somewhere in between, half-way. The Spaniards and Portuguese were haughty and arrogant colonizers, but on the other hand they had a free and easy relationship with the women of their colonies, and treated their illegitimate children well. It all has something to do with the quality of the women, it seems. Given the broadmindedness of the French coupled with the beauty of Tahitian women, and all race-problems were solved here before they became apparent.

If you ask a Tahitian woman whether she is married, she will probably say yes and that means she is living with a man.

When she has gone through a marriage ceremony, she will say she is married-married. (Tahitians never thought much of the ceremony but in certain cases, particularly when inheritance of land is involved, married status is of importance.) In a land where all Europeans were married to Tahitian women, Europeans had no chance – if they had wanted to – of remaining aloof and keeping their distance.

The most extraordinary race relations are those of the Chinese. Almost everywhere else these able, honest and like-able people are regarded as the Jews of the South Pacific, something of a necessary evil. They run all the shops, gain great economic influence and are generally detested. As a result of this – and also for other reasons – they keep to themselves, do not mix much with the host-race socially and marry, exclusively, other Chinese. Here 88 per cent of the 10,000

Chinese are Tahiti-born, the rest are mostly the citizens of Nationalist China. It was in 1865 and 1866 that the first Chinese – 1,100 of them – were brought here from Hong Kong, to produce cotton. (During the American Civil War, the American South could not export cotton and prices on the world market quadrupled. So many countries, small and large, tried to produce cotton. Tahiti's cotton-dream was over in a few years but the Chinese remained and multiplied.) Today they run most of the shops, but this is not resented. The Tahitians hate dealing with officials, filling up customs declarations, fighting with bureaucrats about excise duties, and keeping books, while the Chinese love all this, so why not let them do it? Besides, many Tahitians – even if they open shops – get ruined in no time; they are too soft-hearted. Relations come in and buy things on credit which they never pay for: or simply take away goods as gifts and if the shop-keeper refuses his relatives anything, however much they may owe him, he is despised as *méchant*.

The Chinese in Tahiti are not aloof and not isolated, either socially or sexually. They wear Tahitian shirts, play the guitar and chase Tahitian women with the fervour of Europeans, often to the chagrin of an older, squarer Chinese generation. (Tahitian men marrying Chinese women is another matter; such marriages are extremely rare.)

Subduing the French was a comparatively easy task. To make your master your servant is a frequent phenomenon in human affairs. But to make the Chinese play the guitar and not only marry, but often marry-marry Tahitian girls, is clear proof that this island has a secret.

*　　*　　*

The island has, in fact, two secrets. It was by chance that I came across the first of these. Everybody told me I must see a *tamure* – that twist-like, very sexy Tahitian dance – and indeed I saw quite a few *tamure* festivals later. But my first encounter with it was a lucky one.

I was walking in a field, outside Papeete, when I heard

drums and singing. I went towards these sounds and found a group of dancers, rehearsing for – as I later learnt – a tour of the United States that included Las Vegas. The dancers wore dirty creased shorts and shirts or overalls – in other words they were dressed as artists dress for rehearsal all the world over. They were semi-professionals, led by a man of great talent and grace. The dance was captivating: it lacked the grotesqueness of Negro convulsions, the sad ferocity of the Cossack gopak or the monotony of Spanish dances. And the most striking feature was that these people obviously enjoyed what they were doing: believe it or not, they *liked* dancing. I had never seen artists who actually enjoyed rehearsing. They radiated joy of life and

joy of dancing, yet concentrated on their work with almost religious zeal.

Next to me there sat an old man who started talking to me in a thin elderly voice, but as he spoke half French, half Tahitian, we could not make contact. Then a rest-interval came and my old friend stood up. He could hardly walk, yet he began to dance. The musicians liked his solo and laughed, they strummed their guitars, beat their drums and played for the old boy. People began clapping: '*Le vieux*! . . . *le vieux* . . .' they shouted and he went on and on. There was nothing comical or self-mocking in his performance: he danced with dignity, concentration and seriousness.

And this is one of the Tahitian's secrets. They enjoy life as it comes and have no further ambition. This lack of ambition is even more important than their capacity for enjoyment: lack

of ambition is three quarters of the way to happiness. They have
to enjoy life with avidity, indeed greedily, because their lives are
shorter than most peoples. Girls of thirteen go and live with
men and their prime does not last long. I heard a young
Tahitian girl referring to her sister as 'elderly'. The age of this
elderly lady was twenty-six. There is a Tahitian saying:
yesterday is gone, tomorrow belongs to the Gods but today is
yours. It is not hedonism but wisdom to live up to this. And
the wisest among them – such as *le vieux* who sat next to me
during the rehearsal – make even more of it: they still know
how to dance when they have forgotten how to walk.

* * *

The second – and better-known – secret of Tahiti I have
mentioned already; it is the *vahine,* the women. I have said –
and thousands of men have said it before me – that they are
beautiful. On second thoughts they are not. They are rather
small; they have flat noses; their faces radiate life but lack
intelligence. Yet they are sexy, desirable and cat-like; their
coffee (or rather capuccino) colour is most attractive and their
eyes are magnets. And their greatest attraction, the pillar of
their fame, is their attitude to life, sex and love. Europeans
settling on the island (or just visiting) used to ask girls of
thirteen or fifteen to come and share their abode. The girl
moved in, she cooked, they made love, she did everything for
the wonderful, godlike European male, and when he had had
enough of her and sent her back to her family, she went without
murmur or rancour. Neither her mother nor she, herself, felt
it unjust to be sent home after two weeks, two months, or two
years. That was the way things were.

In Tahiti sex was not connected with sin. The missionaries
tried to persuade Tahitians that the sexual act was something
awful and reprehensible, but they achieved only moderate
success. For the Tahitians, sex is there to be enjoyed; it is an
impulse, like hunger. When you are hungry, you eat. A
Tahitian girl may be very shy in walking into a restaurant or
posing for a photograph, but she will find it most natural to ask

175

you to come home with her after dinner. And when she suggests this – or accepts your invitation with a happy smile – she does not pretend to believe that she is going to see your etchings. She is inviting you to sleep with her and enjoy it. The sexual act is no great emotional event; it is functional, not emotional, and as for the missionaries views about sin . . . well, quite a few of the missionaries were invited as well.

This idyllic situation, the easy procurement of temporary Tahitian wives so convenient for visiting and immigrant Europeans, is almost over. It was the eternal law of supply and demand that changed it. I was referring to this sad phenomenon when I said earlier that the presence of the French military, if unlikely to change the nuclear balance of the world, has certainly changed the sex-life of Tahiti. After the end of the war in Algeria, about 8,ooo hungry males – many of them members of the Foreign Legion – invaded the island and started a keen search for women. Slowly the girls became aware of their value: they are more demanding and more choosy than before. They want to ride scooters and drive motor-cars; they want to be taken for a trip to Paris. In other words, they are getting ambitious, which is a small tragedy for the French military and a great tragedy for the women themselves.

*   *   *

'Tahitian women make the most superb wives in the world.'

An elderly Spanish gentleman, Francisco da Pinilla, explained this to me, drink in hand, in his beautiful garden. He used to be a high official of the United Nations – far up in the World Health Organization – but chucked it all, said goodbye to the UN and World Health, came to Tahiti, married – just married, not married-married – a Tahitian girl and lived with her for thirteen years.

'They are wonderful,' he continued, 'but not for the reasons that silly ignorant Europeans expect. They are not obedient, timid little creatures. They are self-willed, they run the house and they are bossy. Then they are maddeningly independent, too. They do not read; it is difficult to have an intelligent chat with them. They go to the cinema for four hours, without even telling you. Or they may go home to their mother for two days; possibly – although only very rarely – to another man. They simply do not understand your worry, anxiety or anger. They find nothing odd in this. Their language – related to Maori – has no word for *fidelity*; and – to their eternal glory – it has no word for *bastard* either. A child is a child. Fidelity or no fidelity, they are adorable. Not only beautiful – although their beauty should not be dismissed too lightly. But they are warm and human. And they never fuss. They ask no questions. They do not ask where you have been; they do not ask whether the electricity bill has been paid. They do not care. They never nag; they never worry; they never complain. They do not pester you by asking if you love them. They never quarrel. Occasionally they throw an ashtray at you but they are never really tiresome. If you've had enough of them, you send them away and they'll go, not only without fuss, without a scene, but even without the slightest resentment. She is over and you pay no alimony.'

* * *

Tahiti, as we know, is also Gauguin's island. It was Gauguin, after all, who put Tahiti on the map. There is no sign of Gaugin's house: huts do not last that long in Tahiti. But there is an interesting Gauguin Museum near Gauguin's former abode in the Papeari district. The Museum does not possess one single original Gauguin – only copies. The last original Gauguin was discovered on the island and bought for a song by Somerset Maugham who, in gratitude, offered a signed copy of *The Moon and Sixpence* to the Gauguin Museum. There is a map in the Museum, showing where the original Gauguins are to be found all over the world; a lot of his letters, articles and notes are displayed, also his books and personal property. Gauguin is not really remembered – after all he died in 1903 – but widely known. Those few who actually recall him – or who heard descriptions of him from their parents – speak about a grumpy old man, ill-tempered and rather

177

unhappy. In his lifetime his paintings fetched about a 100 francs apiece; today they change hands at upwards of £100,000.

But the reasons for his unhappiness were financial only to a small extent. He was chasing a dream and he could not find it. Tahiti was not primitive enough for him – not even in those days; it was too sophisticated, its food was too French and the girls, bullied by missionaries, started wearing long frocks instead of the *pareu*. It is rarely mentioned – and certainly never in Tahiti – that Gauguin, despairing of finding his dream, left Tahiti and died in the Marquesas.

And this brings me to the last important aspect of Tahiti. The place is not only an island; it is also a dream. People who have been chasing dreams vainly all their lives, come to Tahiti. Some lie to themselves and try to believe that they have found it; others, like Gauguin, leave the island and continue the hunt for happiness elsewhere.

I was sitting in the bar of a hotel with my friend, the former tycoon of the World Health Organization, Francisco da Pinilla, when we became aware of a gentleman, speaking in a loud, American voice. He had just received his bill.

'How much?' he shouted thickly. '341 francs?'

He told a dirty story: no one laughed. He shouted at the Tahitian bar-girl but she was talking quietly to someone else.

'I've got to go home to the wife,' he shouted without moving.

'It's a Tahitian wife,' Mr da Pinilla whispered to me.

'341 bloody francs, eh?' he shouted again. He handed the money to the girl. One of the hundred-franc notes was torn and the bar-girl handed it back.

'No bloody good? It *is* good. Bloody good money. Who wants another drink?' No one stirred. 'Come on. I'll stay here till Christmas, if you want me to, standing drinks to the whole bloody lot of you.'

There was silence. The girl, at last, said something to a waiter in Tahitian.

'Speak English. Don't give me your bloody lingo.' He sounded angry. He fell silent for a short while. Then he said with a feeble smile:

'I must go home to the wife.'

178

And went, with uncertain steps.

Da Pinilla remarked: 'Another Tahiti dream gone wrong. The place is full of them.'

'What about you?' I asked him.

'Me?' he sounded surprised. 'I have a vague suspicion that I am happy. I feel guilty for being happy, of course. What right do I have to be happy in this world? I am still faced with a few questions one cannot answer in Tahiti any more than one can in the United Nations Building in New York or at Piccadilly Circus. But, on the whole, I love this life, I love this island, I am rejuvenated here and happy. Do you believe me?'

'Yes, I do. You are happy, because this happiness is in you. People can't catch happiness by chasing it. You have found it because it is hidden in you.'

He looked at me, stupefied.

'You mean that I am not the only living exception? That I am not the one man who has succeeded in making the Tahitian dream come true? You mean,' and his voice trembled slightly, 'that I would be just as happy in my dull, administrative job in the World Health Organization?'

I nodded.

He looked at me with disgust. Then he said: 'Damn you. You are right.'

BRITISH: Fiji

The island of Fiji was put on the map – as far as the general public is concerned – as an international Clapham Junction, a global Crewe. People did not exactly have to change at Fiji, but planes between Australia or New Zealand and Los Angeles or San Francisco stopped there. There is a great deal of snobbery involved in knowing the names of places like Fiji: the casual name-dropping of these international stops surrounds you with a cosmopolitan halo. Their fate varies as much as the fate of human beings. In the early days of transatlantic travel, Shannon in Eire and Gander in Newfoundland were dropping from everybody's lips. But with the lengthening of the range of modern aircraft, Shannon and Gander faded out, just as – with the decline of rail travel – Crewe itself is slowly fading. Fiji has been luckier. Fiji is still going almost as strong as Clapham Junction itself.

Tahiti was put on the map by Gauguin; Fiji by Qantas and Panam. This is not the only difference between the islands. Indeed, you are surprised how two neighbouring islands can be so different. The word 'neighbouring' should be understood, of course, in its South Pacific sense. They are next-door neighbours in the same warm blue waters, which means that they are not much further away from each other than London is from Moscow or from Cairo.

The Tahitians and Fijians look very different from one another. The Tahitians are Polynesians, the Fijians are Melanesians, which means that the Tahitians are lighter in hue and the Fijians much darker, with more negroid features and fuzzy hair. If the women of Tahiti are unforgettably beautiful, it is the hefty, well-built men of Fiji who leave a strong impression on the mind. (Indeed they do; a great many ladies from California keep coming back to the islands, accompanied by their husbands, or alone.) The Tahiti Group – the Society Islands – consist of a mere hundred and thirty islands, Fiji has more than three hundred and fifty. Tahiti has 84,000 inhabitants, Fiji almost half a million. The Tahitian language is related to Maori, Fijian is a Melanesian language. The tribal system is losing more and more of its significance in Tahiti, while the chief is still a dominant figure in Fiji's social and political life. Tahiti is a French 'territory', Fiji is still a British Crown Colony. In Tahiti one drives on the right, in Fiji on the left. In Tahiti one keeps on seeing the peculiar, high caps of French officers, while the Fiji policeman presents a very different picture: his face is black; his torso is covered with a British-type police tunic; and from the waist downward he wears the *sulu*, the Fijian skirt – or perhaps one should call it the Fijian version of the sarong or the kilt.

Not that it was so very easy for Fiji to become a British colony. Nowadays it takes much less effort for any small island to stop being a British colony than it took for Fiji to become one. Cakobau, King of Fiji, made an application to Britain in 1871 to be accepted as a colony, but his application was turned down. Then he asked the United States but was no luckier. Feeling downhearted ('nobody wants me' is as depressing a feeling for a would-be-colony as for a child) Fiji re-applied to Britain in 1874. This time Victoria's maternal heart took pity on the unwanted island and the small jewel of Fiji was added to her crown.

And yet nearly a hundred years of British rule did not make Fiji as British in atmosphere and appearance as a shorter period has made many other colonies. In Tahiti you are unmistakably in the South Pacific and you could not possibly be anywhere else; but walk around in certain areas of Suva or Nadi in Fiji, and you will think yourself in the Middle East or India. You find bazaars, with all their riches and filth, with all their colour and noise; you start *smelling* people; you see mothers carrying their children on their backs; you see women in the sari and men with the fez; you are pestered by beggars – you had not seen one of them in Tahiti; and the faces around you are neither Polynesian nor Melanesian but Indian.

In fact you have come across the grave – and unique – problem of Fiji. Here the natives of the island are outnumbered by the immigrants. Fiji eighty-nine years ago had not seen one single Indian. After their arrival the British slowly discovered that the Fijians, charming and lovable people though they may have been, were no devotees of working on the sugar plantations. Why anyone should *like* working on sugar plantations – it is hard, back-breaking, degrading and dehumanizing work – is a question which does not concern us here. (Why, for that matter, should anyone *like* coal-mining or brick-carrying? Yet another question, and one which concerns us even less.) Whatever the answer to these questions, the Fijians hated and avoided work on the sugar plantations and the new masters, five years after signing the Deed of Cession, in 1879, imported indentured Indian workers. The Indians did the work they were supposed to do but they did two further things as well: they soon became the predominant race in the economy of the island, and they also multiplied so fast that today they outnumber the Fijians. In 1965 there were 235,000 Indians on these islands and only 195,000 Fijians, a ratio of 100 to 82.

This situation makes the Fijians feel that they are not masters of their own country, and leads to tension. But Fijians only look fierce and awe-inspiring; in fact they are gentle and warmhearted. The fire-walkers of Beqa Island are symbolic: they walk on glowing embers but they do not get burnt. Similarly, even in the old days of internecine, tribal warfare, pitched battles were fought for days, with more than a thousand warriors taking part on each side, using poisoned spears and arrows and the noise of battle reverberating throughout vast regions of the mountains and the valleys: and the result was something like eight killed and thirteen wounded. They were, as is well known, magnificent fighters; but war is also a game and they like playing. They radiate general warmth: even their war-songs have a quality of friendliness. You watch their warlike dances and discover that those terrifying warriors, brandishing

their spears and uttering savage war-cries, are in fact smiling
sweetly. Their threats sound like loving threats; their war-cries
are endearing war-cries. Their gentleness is one of the reasons
for their lack of success as a race; their very niceness is the cause
of their tragedy. In this respect they remind you of the Indians
of Peru. In this atmosphere, the racial situation causes no
eruptive tension or murderous bitterness; yet it remains serious.

The basic problem – or so it seems at first sight – is the
relationship between Fijians and Indians. The Fijians, not
unnaturally, feel that this is their country, so they should be the
dominant race. There is a doctrine in Fiji, according to which
each race used to make its own contribution: the Fijians owned
the land, the Indians provided the labour and the Europeans

supplied the managerial skill and the capital. Soon after the
arrival of the British, the Indians started buying up the land of
the Fijians and the British put a stop to this: Fijian land (about
85 per cent of all lands on the island) is inalienable now and
must remain the property of Fijians. So if Indians want to buy
land, they must buy it from Europeans. Or else, they must *rent*
it from Fijians. All this does not make the Fijians very happy.
They enjoy the security of the land tenure, there is no doubt
about that. There are a few reasonably rich Fijians in Suva.
But even these so-called rich Fijians have only a fraction of
what European managers or Indian businessmen and industrialists may possess. They can have jobs, often high jobs – but
what can an official earn compared with a successful financier
or industrialist? They can make some money on their land but

not much: they cannot *sell* (the law, as we have seen, forbids selling in their own interest). Agricultural land is no source of great fortunes and they do not participate in the benefits of land-speculation, building operations etc. They only get the agricultural rent and while rents are increasing, one cannot grow rich on them. In any case, the Fijian land-owners are not the Fijian nation: the masses also find it hard to improve their lot, because they, too, refuse to take part in business operations, and prefer to stick to their villages. Consequently Fijians feel that they are doomed to remain the third race – after the Europeans and Indians – on their own island.

The Indians are not much happier. They are shown as the villains of the piece: intruders who grabbed finance and industry, who try to deprive poor Fijians of their land and who are – in any case – an alien race who have nothing to do with the Pacific. This, they point out with indignation, is an entirely false and biased picture. They did not come here as tourists who later, sneaked stealthily into the island's economy; they were brought here by force to do jobs the Fijians had refused to do. This happened almost a hundred years ago, so practically all the Indians were born on the island, indeed, many of them are third or fourth generation Fijians. Why keep up this race-division and why not develop an ideal of common aspirations instead? A Fijian is a Fijian, irrespective of the colour of his skin. It is also unjust, they continue, that the Indians must rent all the land they need; eighty per cent of them are landless farmers. They improve the lands they rent and then, when the lease is up, they are turned out. (There are new laws now, protecting Indian tenants and giving them, provided they pay the rent and keep other stipulations of the contract, very reasonable security of tenure. They get a ten-years lease and they may insist on a second ten-year period. After twenty years they must leave the land, should the Fijian landlord so desire, but the tenants are entitled to compensation for the improvements.)

The Indians' demands – the Fijians and the British reply – sound fair and reasonable on paper. But what would they mean in practice? 'Fijian national conscience', talk of 'common aspirations and destiny' – such phrases sound fine but if the

Indians were allowed to buy up the land, they would do so in a short time and the Fijians would still be poor *and* landless into the bargain. Such a situation would surely lead to riots and disastrous race relations.

The Indians reject these counter-arguments. The only serious race-riots in Fiji (in 1958, during a strike of oil-workers) were not between Fijians and Indians but between Fijians and Europeans. Besides, they say, observe what ludicrous results these definitions of race lead to. To be able to speak of 'Indians' and 'Fijians', these notions have to be defined. An Indian is a person who is the descendant of an Indian immigrant. Further, an Indian immigrant is a person who belongs to the Aboriginal races of the subcontinent of India. Fijians, on the other hand, are the natives of Fiji *and the South Pacific area*. The result of this definition is that any Tahitian, Samoan or Solomon Islander who cares to come to Fiji is regarded as a Fijian in the first five minutes of his stay; but an Indian, whose great-grandfather was born in the islands, is not a Fijian.

*   *   *

As always, a large number of people blame the British for the trouble and, as always, they are to some extent right. There is little doubt that the British, by securing ownership of the land for the Fijians, did a great service to the natives of these islands; there is even less doubt that the British have enjoyed and exploited the racial tensions which made a divide-and-rule policy feasible, indeed easy. They hold the press and radio firmly in their hands and these organs are in the service of the establishment, and concerned to preserve the *status quo*. The press and radio wish to maintain European economic power and 'European' in this sense means 'Australian', because banking, gold, copra, and above all the all-important sugar-refineries are in Australian hands – are Australian monopolies, in fact. (The alternative would be Indian economic power – not Fijian.) The opposition points out that even the so-called protection of Fijian land has benefited Europeans just as much as, or more than, Fijians. In the late eighteen-seventies and in the early eighteen-eighties (before the Indians appeared on the scene as an economic power), the British bought Fijian land for a song. They obtained some 400,000 acres. Afterwards, the White Settlement League, bent on maintaining white power, wanted to encourage European immigration and, as a result of their pressure, the land-laws were relaxed: Fijians were allowed to sell their land but only to Europeans not to Indians. Since very few Europeans immigrated to Fiji it was the local Europeans who took advantage of the new law and bought a lot more land from Fijians. Today, Indians can buy land from Europeans but not from Fijians and this arrangement, of course, puts a premium on European land and keeps prices very high. The opposition regards these British manipulations with grave suspicion. The British have learnt nothing, they say. It is still the Colonial Office that rules Fiji (even if it is now accommodated under the roof of the Commonwealth Office and goes under fancy names). When there is trouble, they maintain, the British make concessions; when things are going smoothly, they do not really care.

A reception in Government House looks as if it were being held in a white colony or in London itself. Eighty or eighty-five per cent of the people are white, half of the rest are Fijians, and half Indians with one or two Chinese thrown in. (The 5,000 Chinese of Fiji are – amazingly enough for these parts – left out of the racial game. They are very reserved, politically inactive and look inscrutable. They work hard, as they do everywhere, and do not even voice their political views.) The Governor himself is a popular and good man who would like to change the racial mixture at his receptions – but, he says, he cannot: this, in a country, where out of 470,000 people only 11,000 (less than 2·5 per cent) are Europeans. With the 13,000 part-Europeans thrown in, their total amounts to 5 per cent. There is great dissatisfaction, too, with the old type of colonial official, who is regarded as condescending and patronizing. Such officials mix with the Fijians and Indians, accept their invitations to their houses if they must, but would not dream of inviting an Indian or Fijian back to *their* houses. The idea simply does not occur to them.

The only – and not inconsiderable – bright spot in the British picture is the arrival of a new type of British official. They started coming in the early fifties and people of all classes and races sing their praises. They are interested and involved; they are friendly but not condescending; they care for the islands; they mix with Fijians and Indians on an equal basis: they even return invitations and are indeed, delighted to have Fijian and Indian friends in their houses. Some of the modern business-men – Australians and New Zealanders mostly, but a few British among them – seem to have the same mentality and treat everybody else as equals. This is an encouraging sign. But the businessmen are 'only' businessmen and the 'new type of British official' occupies junior posts only. The tone is still set by their seniors who have never heard that Palmerston is dead.

*   *   *

Tensions exist but race-relations are far from explosive. The British have a fair – and probably equal – number of sycophants among both races. The opposition is most critical about the hereditary chiefs who, wishing naturally enough to keep their own power, consequently support the *status quo* and are in favour of British rule. There are no clashes between Fijians and Indians because there is little contact. Until very recently (1966) Fijians could not leave their villages without the chief's permission; and prior to 1920 – as a result of their indenture system – if the Indians left their places of work they could be prosecuted. In other words, the two races were kept apart – they even had separate schools, so apartheid ruled supreme. By now, these rules have been changed, contacts between the races – mixed schools for example – are encouraged. But policies change faster than life, and the actual rate of change is still very slow. Fijians still live essentially in the villages and it takes a great deal to persuade a Fijian to leave his native village. He might do so temporarily, but having made some money in the town he will return to the village. Indians, on the other hand, live mostly in towns. Social contact between Fijians and Indians is very limited. Religious rules make it difficult for them to eat together and intermarriages are extremely rare – almost non-existent. All that can be claimed is that in Indian districts many Fijians speak Hindi and eat curry, while in copra-country the Indians eat Fijian food and like it. Nevertheless voting is not strictly along racial lines. The Indians complain that as they live mostly in towns, their larger numbers do not secure political advantages for them: they can elect their members with vast majorities, but they cannot elect more members. Yet only seventy-five per cent of the Indians vote for the opposition and one quarter votes for Ratu Mara's Alliance Party (i.e. the Government), and some Fijians vote for Indians.

The political tension is well below boiling point. The Queen is represented by the Governor who is advised by an Executive Council which has a majority of unofficial members. The Executive Council is the Government, the Legislative Council is Parliament. The Legislative Council has eighteen unofficial, and may have up to nineteen official, members – in other words, a majority for official views can always be secured. According to the new constitution it has six Fijian, six Indian and six European members. Everything works towards self-government, but rather slowly: 'when the time comes', 'when the situation is ripe' etc. There are gentle rumblings and some people talk of independence, but even they wish independent Fiji to remain a member of the Commonwealth.

Whether small islands like Fiji should or should not become independent states, is quite another problem. But independence is in the air and I was told that even the Pitcairn Islanders talk of independence. As Pitcairn is a small island, far away from practically everything, and the total number of its inhabitants is eighty-nine, few people encourage these aspirations. This is a pity. Size is relative; Switzerland, for example, is a giant compared with Liechtenstein. The appearance of an independent Pitcairn Island at the United Nations would give status and weight to quite a few independent countries whose present standing is somewhat doubtful.

(Pitcairn Island, if I may digress into brackets for a moment, has graver problems than independence. Its population has fallen from a hundred and fifty-two to eighty-nine in the last ten years and this makes it very difficult indeed – as I read in the *Pitcairn Miscellany* – to play cricket. The truth is that there are now no cricket matches, except occasional games between islanders and visitors. 'How can we become an independent nation,' a Pitcairn Islander visiting Fiji asked me, 'when we can't even put two cricket elevens on the field?' I told him that according to the Charter of the United Nations, this was not an essential qualification. I doubt if the Soviet Union could put two cricket elevens on the field.)

* * *

Fijian villages are still run by the hereditary chiefs whose prestige, if slowly declining, remains high enough. If a chief is rich, he is respected; if he is poor, he is not. (Which proves that Fiji is fast approaching – indeed has already reached – the high level of European and American moral standards.) In the old days, to mention only one example, the chief could command free labour from villagers to do various chores – building, repairing – or simply domestic duties in his house. Today these rights no longer exist and the chief has to pay the villagers; but few people know about their rights and if the chief commands, they obey. The truth is of course, that few people *want* to get rid of the chiefs' protecting, paternal powers. Freedom means responsibility and people prefer to leave responsibility to the chief. For many a new state, colonialism was a disaster but freedom was worse. So many Fijian villagers, anxious not to learn anything about their newly won rights, go on obeying the chief.

Village life is a hand-to-mouth existence but no one has to starve and life is reasonably easy; and certainly very quiet. So it flows on. If you visit a Fijian village and you are lucky, they will throw a *kava*-ceremony in your honour. *Kava* (also called *yaqona* – pronounced *yanggona*) is the national drink of Fiji. You sit down in front of a *tanoa* (a wooden bowl with legs – in case your Fijian is not quite as good as mine) and you will get a *bilo* (cup) in a coconut shell. You sit cross-legged and clap twice.

The chief will cry *maca*; you do not say *maca* yourself. You say nothing, just drink your *kava*.

The Fijians allege that *kava* is made from huge pepper-roots and is slightly intoxicating. In fact it is not intoxicating at all and it is made from mud. It also tastes like mud, which is not surprising in the circumstances. Fijians tell you with a modest smile that *kava* – or *yaqona* – is an acquired taste. But this is a mistake and there is no need for them to be so reticent and modest about it. It is not an acquired taste at all. If you like mud, you will instantly like *kava*.

*   *   *

1968 will be an important year: it will mark the hundredth anniversary of the last occasion on which a missionary was eaten on the island – actually in the village of Nabutautau. He was the Rev Thomas Baker and after so many years his tragedy has become a funny story in Fiji; but there is more to it than meets the eye. The Rev Baker was cooked and the chief wanted to eat a leg. Finding it very tough he sent it back to the kitchen. But no amount of boiling made it tender. Then another missionary arrived and suggested modestly that perhaps it might help if the Rev Baker's shoes were removed. Today the villagers of Nabatautau are not at all ashamed of their ancestors' cannibalism but they are very touchy about the culinary blunder their chief committed.

Why, if the Rev Baker was eaten, was the other missionary received in such a friendly manner and allowed to draw attention to the chief's mistake? The answer is that cannibalism was already on the decline in Fiji a hundred years ago and the Rev Baker had rather bad luck. He was initially well received by the chief, offered hospitality and put up in a *bure* – a Fijian hut – for the night. The Rev Baker, however, possessed a beautiful tortoiseshell comb and it was this possession of his that sealed his fate. The chief came to his hut in the morning, accompanied by two of his bodyguards, armed with clubs. The chief's eyes fell upon the comb. He picked it up and began to comb his hair but could not do it properly because his hair was too thick. So the Rev Baker, politely and helpfully, tried to show him how to do it and started combing the chief's hair. Upon which the two bodyguards fell on him and clubbed him to death. Once he was dead, they thought they might as well eat him.

This was because one of the strongest taboos of old Fiji was that a chief's head must not be touched. It was a heinous and unforgivable crime, and even death was insufficient punishment. The Rev Baker was not eaten simply because he was dead; it was one of the laws – based on deep moral conviction – that such a grave crime could only be expurgated if its perpetrator was eaten up and thus completely annihilated. The Rev Baker committed a fatal mistake – but all that followed was strictly within the rules. The Rev Baker had his set of dogmas; the Fijians had theirs.

*　　*　　*

But the days when Fiji was known as the Cannibal Island are gone. Civilization, as usual, started with turning the spoken language into a written one. Missionaries, as is often the case, did a much better and more useful job in the cultural field than by saving souls. In Fiji, however, they met with a unique difficulty – and the results survive to this day. The language was so full of *mb, ng* and *nd* sounds that the primitive printing sets available on the islands just did not have enough *ms* and *ns*. So these letters were simply left out and the rule drawn up that *b* read as *mb*, *d* as *nd*, *g* as *ng* and *q* as *ng-g*. We have already met the word *yaqona* (pronounced, I repeat: *yanggona*); *Bequa* – the firewalkers' island – is pronounced Mbengga and Sigatoka is Singatoka. Today this shortage of *ms* and *ns* is no longer so acute, yet the rule survives. The French spell Nadi – the airport town – *Nandi,* the British still stick to *Nadi* but both pronounce the name of the town *Nandi*. One might have hoped here was at least one issue on which the British and the French could agree; but this was not to be.

By the way, I got into one of the gravest linguistic embarrassments of my life in that town of Nadi. I wanted to spend a penny (and a real penny, because the currency is exactly like ours) and strolled in the right direction in a restaurant. But what do you do when you see the word *Turoga* on the door? I admit that there was a skirt painted on the other door, which would be a help in any other country. But which door – I repeat, which door – do you choose in a land *where men wear skirts?*

*　　*　　*

Today Fiji is a superb holiday resort, the two largest islands, Viti Levu and Vanua Levu, holding as much attraction for the visitor as the enchanting smaller islands. Yes, the place is magnificent – with one serious drawback. Fiji is a free port and almost everything is ridiculously cheap. You see scores of Americans – some people of other nationalities, but mostly Americans – roaming Suva's Indian shops, hunting for hidden treasures. This they do because they are sportsmanlike: otherwise, not much hunting is needed and the treasures far from being hidden, are displayed only too conspicuously. Prices are staggeringly low, nay: irresistable. And this very cheapness makes Fiji one of the most expensive countries in the world. By the time you have bought an unnecessary camera with two even more unnecessary extra telescopic lenses, two tape-recorders, five bottles of perfume (*really* dirt cheap), half a dozen lighters, a cashmere stole with traditional embroidery, three agate necklaces and four amethyst pendants, you find that all this adds to the bill.

AUSTRALIAN: Papua-New Guinea

How to Get There is the routine opening phrase of conventional travel guides and a very pertinent question it is in the case of New Guinea. The first thing to do is to get a travel permit before leaving Australia. You need a permit not only if you are an alien, not only if you are a citizen of the United Kingdom, but even if you are an Australian. Papua-New Guinea is Australian territory (the exact position will be explained later), yet an Australian citizen needs a permit to get from one part of his country to another. I asked one of the highest officials of the Australian Government dealing with this Territory why this was so.

'We must make travelling difficult,' he replied, 'in the interest of the natives. If it was too easy to travel, they would come over to Australia, wander around here hopelessly, starve without jobs, in utter despair. We must save them. We must protect them. Travelling has been made difficult in their own interest.'

This is a noble motive. But it fails to explain why it is so difficult for Australians to get into New Guinea. They do not wander around there hopelessly, without jobs and in utter despair. Why did *I* need a permit? I wanted no job, had enough money to keep myself and needed no protection. One hears, however, of cases when permits are refused to people with reputedly liberal views – such as Professor Max Gluckman, the British anthropologist.

What to do on arrival? On arrival – from one part of Australia to another – you have to go through customs. Your bag will be thoroughly searched, practically unpacked, by white customs

G   193 officers. Not one New Guinean has been found suitable to perform the complex and highly intellectual job of a Customs Official.

Eventually, I reached my hotel. It was one of the two best hotels in Port Moresby, and that means, in the Territory. It looked frightening at first sight but on closer acquaintance it turned out to be much more frightening than it looked. The heat was stifling, the room was an oven and – this was the first thing I noticed – there was no air-conditioning. Then I noticed a few more things; for example that there was no wash-basin in the room either. I went down to the lobby – a dreary, noisy, dirty place – and asked the receptionist if there were any air-conditioned rooms with bathroom in the hotel. She said no and gave me a look as if I were a raving lunatic. Had I asked her if it was allowed to shoot passers-by from the window, she could not have looked at me with greater astonishment. I started making a few phone-calls from a coin-box (the only telephone at the guests' disposal) and, between two calls, I heard my name on the loudspeaker. At first I thought someone was calling me back, but it turned out to be the receptionist informing me that another gentleman was to be moved into my room. Slightly taken aback, I murmured something about my room having been booked weeks before by an Australian official body, whereupon she told me: 'It's only one other man.' Seeing that I deemed one other man one too many, she informed me that I could have a room 'all to yourself' in the annex. I was taken over to the annex through a ghastly passage which smelled of rats and other unpleasant things and led into a cell, twice as hot as my former oven. I returned to the main building in a thoughtful mood. I was informed that I had been reprieved, the gentleman in question would be put into somebody else's room and I could stay on my own 'for the time being'.

'But that's quite normal,' another guest, a frequent visitor to Port Moresby, explained to me later that evening, over a glass of beer. 'Sometimes four or five people are put into the same room. Two sleep in beds, the others on the floor. There is no real competition between the two top luxury hotels here, so they do as they please. Besides, there is a genuine shortage of accommodation.'

'But if this is the case,' I asked, 'how do the native people live? The Papuan employees of hotels, restaurants, shops?'

'You can imagine. Even clerks employed by the Government often occupy some of those card-board boxes on the hillside. People who live in houses are five or six to a room, three to a bed. Hotel employees, as likely as not, live in the snake-pit.'

'Snake-pit?'

'Sure. They are thrown on top of each other. Like snakes. That's why we call it the snake-pit.'

*   *   *

I went down to dinner. The waiters were wearing the *lap-lap*, a kind of white sarong covering the lower part of their body and leaving the upper part completely bare. They were also bare-footed and called *boys*. (All native males, irrespective of age, are *boys*.) You had to order your dishes by number. There was a choice of about five or six dishes altogether, but, apparently, to say 'soup, please' instead of 'Number One', would be beyond the grasp of the native waiter. The 'boys' were all sullen; you could feel the cool hatred in their hearts. There was no smile on their lips either; they seemed to have forgotten how to smile.

Next morning a boy knocked at my door at 6.30 and asked me if he could do my room. I asked him to come back a little later, say after seven. But I had to be down to have breakfast at seven o'clock precisely, he told me, and my room *had* to be empty before seven. By order of the management. So all guests tramped to the washroom – the type of place used by the Turkish army in the days of Lawrence of Arabia. Guests queued up for showers and for basins to shave. When I got downstairs, I saw some of the waiters arriving in the dust-cart. Half of the lorry was occupied by rubbish, rotting cabbage leaves, potato peel, fish bones and empty beer cans; the other half by our waiters. They tried to keep in a corner, away from the putrid rubbish and the thousands of flies feasting on it. The boys were all clean and decently dressed, in shorts, shirts and sandals. Most of them wore good watches on their wrists. They jumped off the dust-cart to appear a few minutes later bare-footed and in *lap-lap*, to serve our breakfast, which we had to order by number.

*　　*　　*

New Guinea is the world's second largest non-continental island. It covers 330,000 square miles. It is a hundred miles north of Australia from which it is divided by the Torres Strait. Politically it consists of three parts: the former Dutch New Guinea (152,000 square miles) – for long a bone of contention which used to threaten the peace of this area if not of the world – is now called West Irian and belongs to Indonesia. Papua, the southern half of the eastern parts (86,000 square miles) became a British Protectorate in 1884 and was transferred to Australia in 1906. The part now known as New Guinea (the northern half of the eastern parts, covering 92,000 square miles) used to be a German colony and Australia has been running it as Trust Territory since the end of World War One, originally on behalf of the League of Nations, latterly on behalf of the United Nations. Papua is Australian Territory, New Guinea is under Trusteeship. The Trust-Territory – about 23,000 square miles of it – consists of a number of islands: New Britain, New Ireland, Lavongai and Manus in the Bismarck Archipelago and Bougainville and Buka in the Solomon Islands. Talking of the Territory, one should correctly refer to it as Papua-New Guinea but as this is a cumbersome name and as the name of the island itself is New Guinea and as the two parts are governed, in any case, as one administrative unit, I shall simply refer to Papua-New Guinea as New Guinea.

The population of the island is 2,150,000 of whom about 20,000 (less than one per cent) are Europeans and 10,000 Asians. The rest are dark-brown Papuans and New Guineans. The population of Port Moresby, the capital, is 42,000. The majority of the people live in scattered villages in the mountains and pursue a traditional way of life which has changed since ancient times in one respect only: many tribes used to be head-hunters and cannibals but these habits are out of fashion now. A man from the Chimbu District told me: 'Some people say that my tribe were cannibals. But a cannibal boils a man and eats him up – all of him. We never ate a whole man, only his limbs: arms and legs. Can you call us cannibals?' I told him the accusation seemed to me nothing but malicious slander.

New Guinea can boast of one of the world's worst climates – tropical, ravaged by malaria, leprosy, tuberculosis and elephantiasis. Villages are isolated, inland communications practically non-existent by road. The only way to get from one place to another is to fly, and as a result of this a great many people who never saw a railway-engine, a refrigerator or an electric razor in their lives, think nothing of boarding an aeroplane and flying a few hundred miles. The island has three hundred landing strips.

Because of the mountainous nature of New Guinea the tribes – both Papuans and New Guineans – are completely isolated from, and often hostile to, each other. There are seven hundred tribal languages spoken on the island and very few are even remotely related to one another. The languages of even close neighbours may be utterly different. The only common tongue is Pidgin.

*   *   *

New Guinea is not a colony, it is a Territory. But the uninitiated observer can be easily misled into believing he is in a colony. Australia does not really *want* New Guinea and gets little joy out of it; for all her difficulties and troubles, she gets mostly abuse and criticism. She could not rob New Guinea of her riches and treasures even if she wanted to because New Guinea has no riches and treasures. The place costs Australia a lot of money. (In fact, it costs now 90 million dollars a year and it was an angry Australian lady who informed me that 'ninety million dollars is a lot of money'. It certainly is for me; perhaps it is even for her. But whether it is a lot of money for Australia to spend on New Guinea is far from certain. Of course, Australia could, in practice, return the New Guinea Trust to the United Nations, grant independence to Papua and wash her hands of the whole business. But there is one overwhelming consideration

'*New Guinea is now being prepared for independence.*'

apart from reasons of prestige which prevents her from so doing.)

New Guinea was occupied by the Japanese during the last war and the Australian mainland was bombed by planes based on New Guinea. Australian forces fought famous battles on the island, and Australia's defence chiefs believe that New Guinea is essential for Australia's defence, particularly as the Northern Territory of Australia is practically uninhabited. Since the end of the war another complicating factor has emerged. Australia could ill afford that Eastern New Guinea – as an independent state – should be closely allied with West Irian and become a satellite of Indonesia. Indonesia may go Communist; at any rate, it is a potentially hostile state of 100 million people which throws covetous eyes at underpopulated, white Australia.

For a long time, Australians used to talk of New Guinea's independence as of something which would come some time in the distant future. There was no great hurry about it. New Guinea has, for example, altogether two university graduates (not counting graduates of its medical school who are not regarded as fully qualified doctors). This phase of Australian policy was called 'gradualism' and it really meant that New Guinea's independence would certainly not come in this century. Perhaps in the next. The United Nations Trusteeship Council issued a report in 1962, followed by another report of the World Bank in 1964. Both bodies criticized Australian policy and after the reports gradualism was given up. New Guinea is now being prepared for independence and a great deal has been done in the last three years. It should be admitted in all fairness that Australia's task is extremely difficult.

A University of New Guinea has been established. For a great number of years it will have more faculty members than students. A number of critics remark that a University is a magnificent idea but what New Guinea needs is not a University but elementary schools. Schools are being built but there is still a grave shortage of school buildings and a desperate shortage of teachers. Many thousands of native children receive no education whatsoever.

The truth is that Australians and New Guineans inhabit two

199

different worlds. In the rural areas – where relationships are always easier – they communicate more with each other, but in Port Moresby and other townships an urban proletariat is developing and these people feel frustrated, angry and humiliated. They resent many things, some of which are small matters which could easily be remedied; others cut more deeply. Some natives – to mention the most trivial complaint – are angry because mountain roads have no footpaths and they have to jump for their lives when Australians drive past in their cars. Others resent the dogs which guard property and are often trained to bite. Others resent the fact that New Guineans are not even registered at birth. When a New Guinean native is mentioned in print, he is described as 'born about 1935' – or whatever the date may be. Take the list of Members of Parliament. The first constituency listed is Angoram, represented by a white man, John Pasquarelli, born on February 15, 1937; the second is Bougainville, represented by a New Guinean, Paul Lapun, 'born about 1923'. All the people of New Guinea celebrate their birthday at Christmas. After Christmas Day they regard themselves as a year older. Again, others resent the *lap-lap* the waiters are forced to wear and the ordering of meals by numbers.

It would be foolish to dismiss all this as trivial. It may be trivial for those who could help this situation, who could alter it but will not; it is not trivial for people who cannot do much about it and who feel humiliated. Humiliation is never trivial. And there are other issues which might well be considered more important. Many New Guineans, for example, resent the fact that Europeans, mostly women, take jobs in the towns which they, too, could do perfectly well. There are too many European shop-assistants, milk-bar attendants, cashiers. The worst cause of resentment – a truly burning issue – is the question of salaries paid to civil servants. Native clerks were getting an annual salary of around £320. It was acknowledged, after long argument, that this was possibly not enough, and that there was perhaps a case here for revision. The revision and arbitration poured oil on the fire. The average increase awarded – after about two years' preponderation – was seventy cents a week (five shillings and sixpence, in pre-devaluation Sterling). Even the most loyal Australian employees with whom I talked and who defended every aspect of Australian policy, told me that this decision was a grave and stupid mistake. New Guineans living on such salaries cannot be properly housed, clad and fed. They live in appalling homes and often do not have enough to eat. Australians, however, often doing the same or just slightly higher jobs, live in luxury. They are better off than the highly paid Australian civil servants of the mainland. They pay no tax, or very little; they get certain extra allowances; they get houses or other accommodation for about £1 a week while in Australia they would spend something like £10 on a house. And even

this is not the whole story: most of the wives take lucrative jobs (as one lady put it to me: 'just to help Harry to pay off the Mercedes'). There is little contact between the races. Many Australians are kind and would like to have native friends. But the natives recoil. Partly they feel very bitter about these matters; but mostly, they feel, they cannot reciprocate invitations. They cannot go to the luxurious house of an Australian colleague and then invite him back to a hut where three people sleep in a bed.

Yes, many Australians try to be kind and helpful. In fact, quite a few feel rather uncomfortable and embarrassed. But others again – not the most educated and perceptive members of the Australian community – behave badly: partly because they are frightened in a strange situation, partly because they are determined to assert their imaginary superiority. A very intelligent New Guinean told me: 'They are a minority and I know that they are the least educated among them; they correspond to the white trash of the South of the United States. But most of our people cannot discriminate. For them they are just "the Australians" and the stupidity and ill-manners of a few spoil relations still further.'

* * *

There is a parliament now in New Guinea. One of the pamphlets says that it is a 'British type' parliament and adds, in the next sentence, that there is no opposition. One is inclined to feel that a parliament without opposition is a Russian type and not a British type of parliament. But this would be unfair; the situation is more complex. Members can speak freely and they can, if they wish, vote against the Government – which is a right certainly not given to members in Russian type parliaments. People occasionally do, in fact, vote against the Government. But they serve the interest of their constituents and they all have frequent favours to ask from the Government on behalf of one or another of their voters. They find themselves on the horns of a dilemma. In order to achieve results and gain benefits for their constituents they must remain on the right side of the Government. That is what they are trying to do. Any criticism is usually prefaced with remarks about their gratitude to Australia and about how aware they are how much Australia is doing for New Guinea. This is a sensible and prudent way of acting, but it is also the way to lose the confidence of a large number of their voters who would like to hear loud outbursts of sharp criticism of the Government and see a determined fight against discrimination. The New Guinea Parliament consists of sixty-four members of whom ten are officially nominated. Ten of the native members are appointed as trainee under-secretaries of state. They are able to observe how a department is run, but they have no power whatsoever. This is one way of preparing some New Guineans for independence and providing future administrators for the country. Whether those people who serve the Australian Government will be trusted when independence comes, is another question.

But independence is not yet knocking on the door. Critics of the Australian Government might argue that in the past Australia failed to do her best to prepare New Guinea for independence; but not even the harshest critic could rightly say that New Guinea is ready for it. Indeed, some New Guineans are afraid of 'premature independence'. They do not want to see chaos, another Congo and the revival of tribal wars. Independence movements are not very strong and vociferous at the moment; there is no explosive tension. But people are morose and sullen, embittered and frustrated. Most New Guineans are fully aware that they owe Australia a lot. They are grateful for material benefits; education could be better than it is, but it would be even worse but for Australian help; Australia cares for the people's health, builds airports and houses, establishes industries and encourages agriculture. Yet society is divided and one cannot help seeing the master-servant relationship between the races.

Some people see a third way out. New Guinea is not ripe for independence, nor can it remain a virtual colony forever. It could become the seventh state of Australia. The idea is occasionally politely discussed in public: more often in New Guinea but sometimes even in Australia. Australian politicians listen politely, nod and murmur things like: 'An interesting suggestion. . . .' Or: 'Hm. . . .' But, in private, I heard both Liberal and Labour members express their views more forcefully and more concisely. They shook their heads and said: 'Never!'

*　　*　　*

One evening, in the garden of my hotel, I talked to the assistant manager of a plantation in the Madang District. He drank seven large bottles of beer while we talked. He was extremely reserved at first but each bottle loosened his tongue.

'We have three hundred of those boys up in Madang. They get sixpence a day. Plus their keep, food and lodging.'

'Lodging?'

'In the snake-pit,' he grinned. 'They are paid about fifteen shillings a month. When they end their contracts – after two years – they get £1 10s for each month they have worked, that is about £36 for two years' work. They also get a *lap-lap,* a towel and their air-fare back home.'

He drank more beer and continued.

'Ours is a coconut plantation. When a boy steals a coconut he is fined £5.'

'But that is four months' wages.'

'Yeah. But they don't have to steal. And they are only fined when they climb up for it. They can take a coconut that's fallen to the ground.'

'Is the £5 deducted from their wages at the end?'

'No. They have to pay cash.'

'But how can they?'

'They always pay.'

He told me that the boys worked in gangs of ten or twenty. The gangs were selected in such a way that friends, or even boys speaking the same language, were never in the same gang. As a rule, members of the gang could not talk with one another. In fact, they often came from mutually hostile tribes and would not speak to each other even if they could. The boys often worked side by side for two years without speaking, or trying to speak, one single word. At the end of the two years they left without saying good-bye, or even nodding farewell.

'I catch them all right when they try to climb the trees. I don't say anything to them. Next day, when the morning line-up comes, the boy will be there. He won't run away, he can't leave the money he's already earned; besides, ours is an out-lying plantation and he couldn't run away in any case. I recognize him – I know them all by name and by face. If I pick on the wrong boy, the others tell me. There is no solidarity between these boys; they give the culprit away. Then I fine him.'

'*You? You* fine him?' I asked.

'Who else? The Chief Justice? Or a magistrate? I am the magistrate. I am the Chief Justice. I am God. Well, it should be the manager, but he prefers to leave this sort of thing to me.

The £5 fine usually does the trick. But if not – or if there is something more serious – the culprit is locked up.'

'For how long?'

'It is not a question of "how long". It's the shame. His *lap-lap* is taken away and his underpants, too, and there he is in the enclosure stark naked. Everybody can look in and everybody does, women too. They all laugh and jeer. That shames him. That is the real punishment. They don't like being shamed, you see.

'They get the strictest punishment for hitting a European. It doesn't happen often but it can happen. If a boy does that, we take him into the office and beat him up real hard. We beat him into a bloody mess.'

'What sort of education do these boys have?'

'None. None at all. They've never been near a school. They are uneducated and illiterate, all of them. But they meddle in politics. Some of them would like to set up a polarian state.'

'What is a polarian state?'

'You must know. Something with a dictator.'

'You don't mean a totalitarian state?'

'Yeah. That's the word. They want to po ... to ... what you said.'

'How is it possible that none of them has been to school at all?'

'I don't know. But I know they must be taught to respect us educated Europeans.'

He stood up. He said he would go to bed now. He bought another four bottles of beer to take away with him for a nightcap. He came to my table for a moment.

'You were shocked when I said we beat hell out of any boy who hits a European. You are a softy. What else can we do? It's hard on us as it is. How the hell could three Europeans manage three hundred natives otherwise?'

I admitted that otherwise they could not do it.

The Finest Country in the World

Australians speaking of Australia, often describe it as 'the finest country in the world'. Some of them smile shyly; others not. Some speak in a jocular manner; others more earnestly. And they all mean what they say.

I am sorry that I had to finish this book with a chapter on Papua-New Guinea which does not exactly throw the most glorious light on the country. Australia *is* a great, a fine country in many ways, growing in importance every year, indeed every month. Her people are kind, simple, jovial, sincere – even if they try hard to look morose, rough, manly and no-nonsense. They hate fuss and are egalitarian in spirit. They are creating a rich, prosperous, splendid land – a new United States, in some ways better than the old one. Everyone can find work in Australia and everyone is decently paid for his work – although some people get more and others less than they deserve. It is a country where one can build an extremely pleasant life for oneself, where the young are healthier and happier than perhaps anywhere else in the world. Outdoor life is not only a pastime, not only a true and delightful pleasure but a bit of an obsession, a mania. What beefsteak is to Argentina, flamenco to Spain, cool reserve and self-control in *all* situations to an Englishman, what vodka is to a Russian and beer to a Bavarian, what money is to a Swiss, that is outdoor-life to an Australian. It is a noble mania, better than vodka, better than cool reserve, better than money.

Nor is Australia the cultural desert her detractors like to picture. It is a young country which has to come up, not only in an incredibly short time, but also the hard way. Even if intellectuals are suspect and have little influence, even if most thoughts and ideas are derivative and imported from overseas, it is not all beer-drinking, football and one-armed bandits in Australia nowadays. There are art galleries, intellectual magazines, excellent modern buildings, concerts, opera houses (under construction) and above all: searching and self-critical discussion, if not exactly general, is at least going on in a growing number of places.

Nevertheless, I feel there are three things Australia could remember with profit. I am fully aware that it may sound a little over-ambitious or worse on the part of a short-time visitor to offer advice to a great and powerful continent. But I feel it is my duty to do so. (Australia is, of course, free to disregard my advice but only at her own peril.)

(1) They must accept that a writer, a journalist, a thinker, a dissenter, an eccentric, a rebel, a critic, a demonstrator can be – I don't say must be, but can be – as important as, and sometimes more important than, a motor-car, a refrigerator or an electric egg-whisk. It is noble and upright to place your trust in God and in the United States. But listening to dissenting views every now and then can't do much harm. Another way of putting the same idea: stop taking yourselves so deadly seriously; and take others – even if they do not sing your praises all the time – a little more seriously.

(2) Tolerance is one of the most shining virtues – the virtue that makes nations truly great. Australians regard themselves as tolerant people because they do tolerate praise, flattery and approval without raising an eye-lid. But tolerance begins at something you dislike: migrants, Asians, Italians, Greeks, Jews, Pommy Bastards, Aborigines, Papuans, critics, left-wingers, artists, non-drinkers. Oh, there are plenty of opportunities to be tolerant. Practice, my boys, practice!

(3) The best way of spring-cleaning is not to sweep things under the carpet and call any man who looks quizzically and critically in the direction of the carpet, a knocker, a twerp, an unpatriotic bastard. You may try to look stern when certain subjects are mentioned and may try to forget them; you may indeed succeed in forgetting them (such problems as White

Australia or New Guinea). Yet, it is not absolutely certain that everyone else will forget them, too. There is just a vague chance that a few people – mostly those concerned – have made a mental note.

I think if these three easy lessons are learnt, Australia, with its vigour, energy, riches, sunshine and relaxed easy manners; with its charming and disarming straightforwardness; with its safe and salutary distance from Europe and the United States; with its paradise for surfers – even with its Surfers Paradise – might become exactly that: the finest country in the world.